A Journey of

Epiphanies

Learning Leadership

By Terry R. Vergon

Title: A Journey of Epiphanies: Learning Leadership
ISBN: 978-0-9894653-0-4

First Edition

Dedication

For my father who taught me a lifetime of leadership by example, for my wife who is my editor and daily inspiration …

… and for those who inspire us to be our best every day.

Table of Contents

Preface

It's funny how life turns out sometimes. As children, we have great dreams and aspirations. As we mature, we find our niche in life when we come across something we like to do or that suits our natural talents. Some of us live out our childhood dreams; some of us find new dreams and enter occupations far different than we expected. I wanted to be an astronaut, then an Olympic skier, and entered college as pre-med. Whether we become teachers, tax auditors, forest rangers, or computer programmers, some of us find our way into leading others.

We are called supervisor, manager, or leader – and in these roles, we can find great purpose in what we do. We use people to accomplish goals. Some of us excel, others survive, and some fail. As a leader, I wanted to excel, and my curiosity drove me to find out what made some leaders successful and others not. I began to study the subject of leadership and found a plethora of interesting, if not bizarre, material – everything from physical attributes and psychological studies to what astrological sign makes good leaders.

In my 30 years of study on leadership, what I did find has nothing to do with astrological signs or physical characteristics – but it has everything to do with what we have realized and discovered about the truths of the human condition. These realizations affect us deeply enough to cause us to look at what we believe and change it. They are surprisingly simple and yet completely profound. They are epiphanies, the milestones in our lives that determine who we are and what we become.

"I took the road less traveled by, and that has made all the difference."

Robert Frost

Chapter 1

Understanding Leadership

I was in grade school. It was early morning, and we had just come in from morning recess. Amid the normal confusion of finding our seats and the teacher trying to quiet us down for the lessons of the day, we heard the first crackle of the school's public announcement system. "Attention. Attention." There was a pause and, even at my young age, I could tell from the strain in the person's voice that something was terribly wrong. "The school will be closing for the rest of the day. President Kennedy has been shot."

My teacher almost immediately broke out in tears and collapsed in her chair. The entire class sat still in the silence of the moment. The assistant principal came in shortly thereafter and told us that our parents were being notified and that the buses would be in their normal pick-up positions in about 15 minutes. When I got home, my mom had been crying and my dad was home from work (very unusual). The television was tuned to the news broadcast from Dallas. It seemed that the whole world was either crying or angry. At the age of seven, I struggled to understand what had happened and was astounded by how it affected everyone *so much*. On that day in November, it was as if the world had stopped – but something had also begun.

As the nation mourned, I began to understand how significant the loss of our president was. I was struck by how much President Kennedy meant, not just to his own family and immediate circle of friends, but seemingly to everyone in the nation. And from then on, the questions that swirled in my mind that day would influence me profoundly. This tragedy created an emotional event in my life which pointed me toward a path of learning about leaders and how they affect us.

I remember wondering through the years: What is it about President Kennedy that could create such a reaction in people who never even knew him? How do some people get to have such power over so many? What *is* leadership, and can anyone be a leader? Why do we follow them? Are we born leaders or is leadership thrust upon us by the situations in our lives?

What *is* Leadership?

According to the dictionary, "leadership" is *"the act or an instance of leading"* (Merriam-Webster.com), but I'd like to expand the definition as follows:

> ***Leadership is acting in such a way as to inspire and help people come together to achieve great things.***

Leaders lead people, not processes or programs or companies. They are experts in human behavior, whether innately or by formal training. They must become experts at influencing, understanding, and observing people. Leaders stand for a specific set of values and beliefs that people connect with and support.

So it follows that, to become a leader, one should focus on acquiring honing these skills and abilities. But in reality, the path to leadership often begins when an individual contributor is promoted to supervisor because of their superior *technical* skills and abilities. There are reasons some people become great engineers and technicians, and I'm willing to bet it isn't to study psychology and sociology.

Leadership is about people and their interactions with others, not about who is the best technically. And in my opinion, the practice of providing a few days of training to an individual contributor and then expecting them to suddenly perform as an expert in human behavior and group dynamics shows a fundamental misunderstanding of what leadership is about and creates many of the problems organizations face today.

It is my greatest hope that this book will help people understand why it's important to change what we look for in leaders, and how we develop and mentor them. After all, leadership is not an "app" that someone adds to their repertoire of skills. It demands much more than that. It actually marks an entirely new direction in their career.

Leadership as a Profession

It's important to recognize that leadership is a profession in and of itself. When you move into the world of leadership, you begin to realize that you have chosen a very different path and that what made you a great technician or engineer will not make you a great leader. In fact, in some circumstances the skills you relied upon before may even become an obstacle to you. In other words, what got you to where you are will not get you to where you want to be.

From the moment you decide to become a leader, you are committing yourself to acquiring a new set of skills and body of knowledge. People become your specialty, and this profession *"… requires considerable training and specialized study"* (The

American Heritage Dictionary of the English Language, Fourth Edition, 2009).

Leadership training and study should focus on subjects such as communication, psychology, sociology, and more. And while these subjects are touched upon in many leadership courses offered today, most company- or corporate-sponsored programs typically don't go far enough to adequately prepare leaders. If you wouldn't consider someone a doctor or engineer after a couple weeks of training, why would you consider someone a leader after a similar effort?

The following is not meant as a compendium but more an overview of the breadth of knowledge that should be acquired and briefly explains how each recommended course of study can assist you on the journey.

• *Communication*

As you might well expect, one of the most important skills of leadership is the mastery of communication. By that I mean that you must learn to create visions in peoples' minds, communicate expectations with unparalleled clarity, and do so in such a manner that everyone who hears you understands exactly what you intend to convey.

Attending communication classes is valuable. Take writing classes, participate in a speech class and practice these skills every chance you get. You can find these types of classes at universities and support groups. Even mentors can help you in this area, but never miss an opportunity to learn more about communication because it is vital to your success.

- *Psychology*

   Since interaction with people is so integral to leadership, it is necessary to learn what makes people who they are and to understand why they do the things they do – and this includes you. Again, go to class, read, and study human behavior. You may manage a large organization, but you inspire one person at a time. Learn what makes us … *us*. Study the Asian cultures and how they develop relationships. Discover that relationships are how we get things done.

   Great leaders understand our needs, the way we look at the world, and how we construct our own realities. The study of psychology can give you great insight into how we relate to the world around us and to each other. Learn how we determine our values and personal culture. Discover what drives us and what is important to us. You cannot lead people without knowing who we are and how we come to understand this world we share.

- *Teaching*

   Teaching others about your vision, your expectations, your hopes, and what you have learned will help you relate to your organization. So I recommend that you take a class on how to teach and how adults learn.

   One of the expectations I set for all my supervisors and managers is that they teach someone something every day. What they teach isn't important. It's just important that they teach. The process of teaching requires that they learn something well enough to be the expert at it. And one of the most important tangible results of teaching is the fact that people naturally come to respect and trust the person who teaches them. So aside from the fact that the overall knowledge base of the organization is increasing, the respect and trust of individuals within the organization is also increasing – and this is very important to leaders, as they must come to be respected and trusted by the people they lead.

- *Organizational Psychology and Group Dynamics*

Leaders must understand how ideas, philosophies, and cultures gain a critical mass and become persistent within organizations, and so another vital course of study to pursue is organizational psychology and group dynamics. As a leader, you must learn how people act and relate within groups, and particularly how they relate to leaders. Again, take classes, read books, and study groups and organizations in action to see how they react, function, and achieve goals.

Leaders must be able to diagnose and address organizational issues such as what makes a group efficient and effective (recognizing that those are two very different things). And they must also understand how groups choose their leaders, because the leader is not necessarily the person sitting in the CEO's chair. Sociology and previously mentioned psychology is where this science and art resides, and near-constant study is required to stay current on this dynamic body of knowledge. Not only does the science constantly evolve, but the organizations and groups themselves are constantly developing in reaction to new and changing cultures being integrated within them. What you learn today may change tomorrow, so keep learning.

- *Business Coursework*

I also recommend taking business classes. You don't have to get your MBA, but it wouldn't hurt. Business classes teach how to measure outcomes, define goals, develop models of behavior, and create plans. It will also help in developing a mode of thinking about problem evaluation and remediation. All of these can be directly or indirectly applied to organizational behavior and help in leadership.

Additionally, understanding finance, resource allocation, and commerce in general will help anyone in the world of business. Many of the concepts around resource flow and exchange are directly attributable to facets of human behavior, which should not surprise anyone as commerce is a human invention to begin with.

- *Marketing, Sales, and the Media*

As the leader, you will be the chief sales officer when it comes to imparting the vision for your organization's future. And at various times in your leadership career you will have to work with the media to communicate and sell that vision. You should know how the media works, why they exist, and how they do their job.

Understanding marketing and sales also helps leaders know how to present ideas in a positive light and how to make them seem desirable. How do you present yourself so that you engender trust and respect? What personal habits do you have that distract from these goals? What changes do you have to make for each audience that you face? As the leader, you are the face of the organization and everything you do is a direct reflection of it. Learn to create and control your image to help yourself and your organization.

- *Business and the Law*

It would be nice to live in a world where everyone perfectly understands what we intend and is honest and forthright; but since we don't, it is necessary to learn about the legal implications of leadership. As a leader, you need to be aware of how your words and actions may actually form a contract, cross a legal line, set policy, or release information that is not beneficial or legal to release. There are many pitfalls a leader can encounter, and the best defense is to learn what these are and how to avoid them. Again, classes, books, and attorneys are all good resources to help you learn about these issues and deal with them.

- *Sociology*

Become a student of culture. In all cultures and societies, there is a proper way to meet someone for the first time. There are accepted norms of behavior while dining, playing sports, drinking, receiving gifts, giving gifts, providing recommendations, and myriad other situations. These norms extend to how we dress, how we talk, when we talk, and even the order of to whom we pay our respect. We live in cultures that have developed these norms of behavior over centuries; and even though cultures are dynamic and do change, it is simplistic to think that we could change these norms overnight simply by wishing they were not so.

If we are to gain respect and trust as leaders, the rules of human behavior require us to give respect and trust. Learning about cultural norms, with the intention to accept and comply with them, is how we start. And since as the leader you are an ambassador of your organization's culture, you must be the example of behavior and respect. Studying culture can help you learn to shape the culture of your organization because everything in an organization is done within the context of its culture.

Don't make the mistake of thinking that simply because you grew up in a certain area means that you know and understand all the norms of the local culture. A culture is simply a reflection of a population's beliefs and values. And as new populations move into an area, bringing their cultures with them, the cultural norms also change to reflect the population's values and beliefs.

Though this list of recommended subjects is incomplete, it helps to illustrate the fact that leadership is actually a profession in its own right with a particular body of knowledge. And hopefully it will help point you in the right direction as you learn the profession.

Leadership versus Management

> *"If you want to make the world's greatest widgets, become an engineer. If you want to make it in the corporate world, become a manager. If you want to change the world, become a leader."*
>
> *Terry R. Vergon*

Stephen R. Covey described leadership and management this way: "Management is efficiency in climbing the ladder of success; leadership determines whether the ladder is leaning against the right wall."

Peter Drucker and Warren Bennis said, "Management is doing things right; leadership is doing the right things." Leadership defines the direction and vision for the future; management finds the most efficient and effective way to get there. Management includes elements of controlling and directing according to most of the definitions I have seen.

But beyond the knowledge and skills mentioned above and the different roles they have within an organization are three qualities every leader must also possess – a strong desire to work with people, a vision, and passion. And it's interesting that managers can be successful without these traits, but leaders will fail if they do not have all three. Let's explore them briefly here.

- *Desire to Work with People*

A strong desire to work with people is what can motivate an individual to change their perspective so they can transition to leadership. And the operative words are "desire" and "with." Leaders do not work *for* people; people do not work *for* leaders – they work together as equals. Each participant contributes, with the leader providing leadership and inspiration. A key attribute of the leader that allows this trait to work is respect – respect for what each person brings to the organization which translates to appreciation.

- *Vision and Inspiration*

The vision the leader brings to the organization is what inspires people. It is an articulated future state which, when compared to the current situation, is desirable and worthy of effort in the minds of the group. The effort people are willing to devote to the vision is directly related to their internal values, personal beliefs and goals, as well as their perception of the social currency to be gained.

First and foremost, the vision must be in alignment with the group's internal values. And this is particularly important to recognize when stepping into a leadership role where the goals of the organization have already been defined. In this case, the leader must understand the organization's values before crafting the vision, and the best way to determine an organization's values is to observe its behavior. While words may reflect an organization's values, they are more often a statement of how the organization wishes to be perceived in the social setting. Actions, on the other hand, come directly from values and are, therefore, a more accurate way to understand what an organization's values are.

- *Passion for Leadership – The Making of an Art*

Without passion for leadership, it is impossible to become a leader. While the benefits of leadership may be powerful motivation for some, anyone pursuing leadership simply to reap the benefits will fall short of the mark and never develop the traits necessary to lead. Instead, they tend to exhibit self-centered or self-serving behavior and quickly tire of the demands of leadership.

Passion for leadership is vital for the person who wants to become a great leader. It becomes the reason they get up in the morning and what drives them to devote the majority of their life's energy to becoming a great leader. It drives an insatiable curiosity about what makes a person a great leader and feeds their desire to become one. Passion is what takes leadership from a series of learned techniques and processes and extends it to an art form.

Leadership is a Learnable Art

Most leadership training programs teach techniques and processes to measure performance, empower groups, and how to motivate people. We learn communication skills, how people relate, how to determine and work with people's strengths and weaknesses, and assess what tendencies people have that influence how they behave. But in and of themselves, all of the knowledge, skills, and tools will not make us great leaders.

That being said, as stepping stones in the journey to becoming leaders, they are invaluable. The knowledge and techniques they provide in understanding human behavior and motivation are critical, and I recommend that those of us on the journey of leadership avail ourselves of as many as possible. Just like an artist, we need our tools or "brushes, paints, and canvas" to create this art of leadership.

Leadership is Learnable

Leadership inspires and helps, but notice that leadership is action. A leader acts to lead. And actions, leading to behaviors, can be learned. Using this line of logic, then, leadership can be learned.

If this is so, then we should be able to identify those behaviors and actions that cause us to become leaders. And one might surmise from this statement that, to become a great leader, one need only observe great leaders in action and mimic their behavior, but this is not actually the case. Leadership, it turns out, is more appropriately compared to playing the violin or painting and, therefore, is more an art.

Expecting to lead by observing and mimicking leadership behavior is akin to recreating the Mona Lisa by learning about colors and shapes and copying brush strokes. While some may be able to reproduce the masterpiece with more than amateurish skill, most would fall short. The difference between amateur and master is that, at some point in their painting life a master had a realization that painting is illusion, which changed their perspective and allowed them to do things beyond colors and shapes.

A similar realization must transform the performance of the violinist beyond learning tone and timing if they are to create the melodic journey the virtuoso can achieve. For the virtuoso, an understanding of how to bathe their music in emotion is what elevates their performances and allows them to reach the audience with such impact.

Leadership is an art, but a learnable one.

I can draw a person and play the trumpet, but not so well as you would want me to paint your portrait or play in your band. The reason for this is that I was just not passionate about learning these arts. The same will apply to you in this art of leadership. Anyone can learn the basics; but to be really good or great, there must be passion. Only those that cultivate a deep desire, passion, and are willing to put in the required practice and effort will become great leaders.

Something is Missing

Passion is good, but even if you are passionate about a violin you might only become a great builder of violins and not a virtuoso. So let's look at what we have so far:

> ***Vision***
> *+* ***Desire to work with people***
> *+* ***Passion for leadership***
> *+* <u>***Skills/knowledge in leadership techniques/behaviors***</u>
> *=* ***Great Leadership Potential.***

Notice that even with all this, we only have the potential for great leadership. Just like with painting or becoming a great violinist, there are realizations or epiphanies about our craft that we must experience. They take us from being mimics of the techniques of our profession to being innovators, creators, and leaders. Epiphanies are the missing piece of the puzzle to becoming a leader. Without these epiphanies, the best that we can hope for is to become great managers. With them, we transform and move beyond our current state to become leaders, just as an artist transforms to become a master or virtuoso.

Epiphanies and Behavior Change

One definition of an epiphany is "*A comprehension or perception of reality by means of a sudden intuitive realization*" (The American Heritage Dictionary of the English Language, Fourth Edition, 2009). For this book, I use the following definition:

> ***An epiphany is that sudden intuitive realization that causes a behavioral change (along with associated values and beliefs).***

Epiphanies change our perception of reality. They often change our beliefs and values. They will change our behaviors. An explanation is necessary at this point to explain how epiphanies change human behavior. This is important as it will have a personal effect on the person becoming a leader and, later, on how the leader can influence their followers.

How do Epiphanies Change Behavior?

There is a definite sequence in the way we change our behaviors. This sequence happens every time in some form, sometimes very quickly -- seconds -- other times over years for more deeply rooted habits. The sequence is always the same:

1. Significant Emotional Event (SEE)
2. Evaluation of our perception of reality
3. Evaluation of behavior options
4. Behavior adoption and expected results

Significant Emotional Event (SEE)

We each have a perception of reality that has been formed over our lifetimes. This perception is developed and added to every day of our lives. Observing and experiencing new and different things adds to our perceptions. As we get beyond our formative years as children, our perceptions become more difficult to change. Our experiences and observations also generally go from formative to supportive of the perceptions we develop.

As we explore how behavior changes, we will talk about a specific situation, the realization that our perception of reality does not match the reality that we are facing. This is the starting point of any epiphany. In this book, we will refer to this situation of initial realization as a Significant Emotional Event or SEE.

> *A SEE is any event or situation that causes us to perform an evaluation or self-examination of our perceived reality.*

A SEE can be as simple as receiving an unacceptable grade on a quiz in school to a truly life-altering event such as surviving a potentially deadly automobile crash. In the workplace, a change in company policy after a sale or merger can provoke a SEE. An individual's threshold for a SEE changes constantly too. What affects the threshold the most is the person's specific situation and experience with that situation.

We've all had different experiences in life that mold our perceptions of reality. In organizations, the leader must know and understand the workforce's social and psychological makeup – its values, cultures, norms, and fears. With this knowledge, the leader can understand a SEE that people are experiencing within an organization or even fashion a SEE to create the opportunity for behavioral change. But in order to successfully affect behavior, the leader must be able to get a critical mass of the organization to experience the SEE.

The SEE forces us to examine what we believe to be true in our world. If it is determined that the situation or observation does not match our perception of reality, we move into an evaluation phase. In a later chapter, we'll look more particularly at how leaders initiate SEEs to change organizational cultures or values and to motivate people; but for now, let's continue to look at how epiphanies change behavior.

Evaluation of the Reality Difference

When we experience a SEE, it forces an evaluation of the new situation. What does this mean to me? How does this affect my world? We look at the new situation as it affects our values and beliefs. Is this something that I need to be concerned with?

This evaluation can have several outcomes. One of the outcomes is that we just do not believe the situation. We choose to ignore it, hope it will go away, and we go on our merry (or not so merry) way. While this may be an outcome, it is normally a temporary path as the situation will continue to work on our subconscience and force some type of resolution.

Another outcome is that we determine that this situation really does not affect us and our behavior does not need to change. This is the case in most situations.

The third outcome is that we evaluate the situation and determine that a change in behavior is needed to respond or compensate for this new understanding of reality, an epiphanic moment. This brings us to the next phase, what to change?

Evaluating Behavior Options

Once we see a need to change our behavior in response to the SEE, we next develop and evaluate possible behavioral changes. We look at what we already do in similar situations or what others around us are doing, and we evaluate what behaviors are needed to develop alternatives. It is during this stage that the leader of the organization can be most influential by providing a model or example of the desired behavior and providing re-enforcement.

Each behavior option is evaluated as it pertains to our desired outcome. We do a cost/benefit analysis on each option: What is the perceived effort or cost associated with adopting the behavior as opposed to its perceived benefits? Remember that benefits can range from monetary to social currency to self-actualization fulfillment. Whichever behavior brings us the most desirable outcome is the one we will choose.

Again, a wise and skilled leader knows and understands their organization well enough to provide models of behavior and a great vision of the future that can influence others during this phase. Great leaders use these opportunities to provide previously unevaluated or out-of-the-box options that stir the imaginations of people and inspire them.

Behavior Modification and Adoption

At this point, we give the new behaviors a try. We evaluate the results, and if they meet our expectations of risk and reward, then we incorporate them into our normal repertoire of behaviors, hopefully becoming "good" habits. If the results do not meet our expectations, then we go back to the previous phase to further evaluate and develop different behaviors.

Leadership should measure the adoption of new behavior within the organization. We do this in schools, the military, and any organization where specific behaviors are important to the success of the organization. As an example, in a nuclear power plant, the leadership measures the number of safety violations and "near-misses" to ascertain whether or not the culture of safety and risk mitigation has been adopted. These metrics are published or made known throughout the organization to reinforce leadership's expectations.

Applying Behavior Change to Our Leadership Journey

Leadership is acting in such a way as to inspire and help people come together to achieve great things; but because this occurs primarily through the agency of change, it becomes very important that leaders have more than an academic understanding of the process. They must have experienced firsthand what it means to change one's own behavior and be comfortable with producing and managing change before they can effectively lead others through change.

By realizing, maybe even self-initiating a SEE, they can learn to change their own conduct, recognizing and seeking out personal opportunities to challenge their own thought processes and behaviors. But because our very nature actively works against change, self-initiating a SEE is difficult at best. Having mentors, teachers, or others that specialize in behavior change around us can help make the journey to leadership less arduous, particularly as we attempt to experience the epiphanies necessary for leadership.

It is also helpful to study other leaders, to learn from their examples and understand how they produce and manage change, and that is why interaction with others in the leadership field is so valuable to those who have decided to pursue the profession of leadership. It is never too late to go back to school, enroll in a class, or attend a seminar. What you are learning is nothing short of a new profession, the profession of leadership.

Of Painters, Virtuosos, Olympic Athletes, and Leaders

I don't care what you do or where you came from; to rise to the pinnacle of your profession you must experience the epiphanies that transform you from being a mimic to a leader.

Jean Claude Killy, a French Olympic skier, at some point realized that doing the same thing as every other skier was not going to help him win races. Mimicking others rarely makes you a leader in anything. He realized, or had an epiphany, that if he leaned back on his skis, this jetted him out of the turns, making him faster. He had discovered how to make the physics of friction and momentum work for him. Many of the journalists at the time called his style "reckless," as it looked like he was out of control as he exited the turns.

In 1968, this reckless skier took gold in all three Olympic alpine skiing events, a feat done only once before and never again and, in so doing, revolutionized the sport of ski racing. His technique reduced his times and increased his speed, giving him the advantage he needed to win.

And so it is for master painters, virtuosos, and people that aspire to leadership. In order to reach greatness, each must experience the epiphanies unique to their field. And just like painters, virtuosos, and Olympic athletes, the journey can be defined by the epiphanies they experience.

A Journey Defined by Epiphanies

> *"Minds are like parachutes; they work best when open."*
>
> *Thomas Dewar*

Learning leadership is like anything else that we must learn – we must first start with an open mind. We have to understand that what we have learned in the past may not help us in the future and may have even been wrong. We will explore more about these traits as we move along our epiphanous road to leadership.

The journey that we take to become a true leader is marked by epiphanies that must be experienced. Just as the painter must realize that they are creating an illusion and the violinist must interject emotion into their performance, leaders must experience certain epiphanies on their journey to becoming great.

Throughout our lives, we experience different revelations about the nature of our existence. But there are certain revelations, realizations, or epiphanies that are common for all within certain pursuits. Like the painter and violinist, leaders have a set of common epiphanies that they must experience. So let's explore these epiphanies to understand what they are as well as how they affect us and the people that we lead.

First Steps

You have applied for it, you have dreamt of the day, and then the day arrives. Ready or not, your boss or manager comes to you one day and says, "Congratulations. We have chosen you to be the new supervisor." Wow, as the wave of euphoria sweeps over you, you realize that you have reached the top of a long hill and triumphed. Amid the smiles and congratulations, you take your place in your new office with its shiny new nameplate and nice chair that soon you will have very little time to enjoy.

As you settle in for your first day, the manager talks to you about goals and expectations and whom to turn to for help. You might even be assigned a mentor. You are told about your new authorities, new responsibilities, and wished good luck, but they are quickly out the door. You are now the supervisor. Now what?

Somewhere between the new supervisor training and the new responsibilities you have been given, you realize that the work you are expected to get done is not humanly possible to accomplish by yourself. Even if you were to work 24 hours a day, 7 days a week, there would be no way to do it all. You must let others do the work. So how do you get others to do the work?

The Leadership Epiphanies

At some point you realize (have an epiphany) that it is necessary to delegate. This is the first epiphany, and it is one that all leaders experience. It is the first step in the path to leadership. Nothing else defines the line between being an individual contributor and becoming a leader. It is also one of the most difficult skills for a leader to master.

In this book, I specifically look at the five major epiphanies that every leader must experience. These epiphanies define our journey. Throughout the remainder of this book we will investigate, explore, and discuss how these epiphanies affect our leadership styles, effectiveness, and success.

As we travel along our leadership journey gaining skills and knowledge, we will continue to experience those "a-ha" moments. Some will provide us insight about our own behaviors, why the organization behaves the way they do, and why our bosses act the way they do.

Four of the major epiphanies will always occur in the order presented. It's like climbing a mountain; it's done one step at a time. The initial epiphany is a gaining of insight that is used to build upon and allows us the ability to experience the next epiphany in the sequence. Just like climbing the mountain, you cannot experience the summit without first enduring the climb and all that the climb entails.

And just like climbing into the high altitudes of a mountain, our behaviors and actions must change to reflect the new environments we encounter. At the beginning of the climb we wear shorts and tee-shirts, casually walking up the well-worn path, occasionally stopping for a rest along the way, but for the most part enjoying a pleasant walk.

As we gain altitude, our clothing changes to keep us warm and dry. Our steps on the high rocky paths are less sure and in some cases missteps have serious consequences. On the high cliffs and glaciers, we rope up for safety, wear our warmest clothing, we rest often, missteps are now possibly fatal, we slow down, double-checking our protection and steps. On the summit, we celebrate, take pictures, snack, and reflect on the view and our journey.

At each phase of our climb, the processes, skills, behaviors, and strategies change. We build upon our knowledge of the new environments; we use new skills and tools to match our new conditions. It is the same with our journey to becoming leaders; we build our understanding and skills so that we may move to the next level.

Just as there are certain milestones in our climb of a mountain, there are milestones that we must pass as we become leaders. In order, the four major milestone epiphanies are:

1st Epiphany: *I cannot do all of the work myself and I must let others do some of it.*

2nd Epiphany: *It doesn't have to be done my way to meet the expectations.*

3rd Epiphany: *These people are actually smarter than I am.*

4th Epiphany: *It's my job to help my people be successful.*

The 5th epiphany can actually occur at any time but usually occurs later in our journey. It is nonetheless a required epiphany.

> *5th Epiphany*: *Influence is all that we really have as leaders.*

In the following chapters, we explore each of these epiphanies, how they affect us, how they change our behavior, and the effect they each have on our organizations.

As with mountain climbing, not everyone reaches the top. Some of us will stop along the way, preferring to enjoy the environment that we are in, not wanting to move out of our comfort zones. Change is hard; moving forward is not always possible for many reasons – some of them self-imposed, some not. The good news is that we all have the opportunity to move in the direction of leadership and participate in the journey.

The journey of leadership is not for the faint of heart. It requires exposure to the new, to unknown challenges, and travel to places we never knew existed. On my journey, I have taken heart in the fact that many have come before and have offered encouragement and inspiration.

> *"The credit belongs to the man who is actually in the arena...who knows the great enthusiasms, the great devotions; who spends himself in a worthy cause; who at the best knows in the end the triumph of high achievement, and who at the worst, if he fails, at least fails while daring greatly, so that his place shall never be with those cold and timid souls who neither know victory nor defeat."*

> *Theodore Roosevelt*

"More power than all the success slogans ever penned by human hand is the realization for every man that he has but one boss. That boss is the man - he - himself."

Gabriel Heatter

Chapter 2

The 1st Epiphany

My father owned a construction company, and I was responsible for various projects and phases of construction. Up until I was sixteen, I took care of these assignments by myself. But everything changed when my father put me in charge of a team of three people, a framing crew. Picture in your mind a teenage boy with no experience in supervision now in charge of three much older, more experienced people.

I was lucky that each of *my* people had at least ten years' experience in construction and didn't actually need a supervisor. I'm sure my father chose them specifically because of this. I believe he thought it would be a safe bet – that with these guys working for me, I couldn't get into much trouble. Boy, did I prove him wrong.

By the end of the first day, there was trouble. I thought that a supervisor needed to tell people what to do, and that's exactly what I did. And my people, being good employees, did exactly what I told them. After all, my father was holding *me* accountable to meet our construction schedules. By the end of the day, I was about a half a day behind schedule and, needless to say, wound up staying late into the evening working by myself to catch up.

Still mystified, the next day my father pulled me to the side and told me I needed to delegate some of the work, that I couldn't do it all myself and I needed to let *others* do it. "You have great people working for you, so let them work for you," was his advice. This was an epiphany for me and I later learned in the Navy that this was "recognizing correct answer when told."

With my father's encouragement and guidance, I learned to work with the team to get the job done on time. I realized that my role as supervisor was to delegate, among other things. This epiphany caused a basic shift in my perspective and behavior, and it was a defining moment. In fact, this first epiphany is what defines the beginning of the path to leadership, and anyone that is put in a position of leadership and responsibility will have this epiphany.

The 1st Epiphany

I cannot do all of the work myself and I must let others do some of it.

The very reason for the supervisor's or manager's position is that there is more work than can be accomplished by one person, and so the group needs someone who can coordinate its efforts to achieve a common goal. But for most people, the 1st epiphany is a pretty scary proposition. It marks the first time in our careers that we no longer have direct control of our results.

We believe *our work* is a reflection of who we are and the basis of how we are perceived by others. When that work is under our complete control, we can take full credit and be proud of the outcome. But if that work is to be done by others and we're still held accountable for the quality, quantity, or both, we naturally want to make sure that it meets our expectations and will reflect well on the image we've created for ourselves. And what's more, as supervisors, we're not measured simply by the quality and quantity of the work performed by our workers. Our ability to manage and lead is another metric that can potentially affect our image in the workplace.

Perceiving that our destinies are in the hands of others is just one of the concerns that translate predictably into behaviors that are commonly seen in supervisors. Another situation with the potential to drive behavior in a new manager occurs when an individual contributor is selected for promotion because of their superior performance record or because they set expectations for themselves and others that are higher than the norm. These can become internal frustrations that set the stage for some of the most common traits seen in supervisors, namely, a reluctance to delegate and micromanagement of work tasks.

Behavioral Traits of the 1st Epiphany Manager

> *"Confidence is the feeling you have before you fully understand the situation."*
>
> *Unknown*
> *(Seen on a shirt in South Lake Tahoe)*

When a person is first put in charge of a group of people, they experience many different emotions. Some of the first are surprise, happiness, and thankfulness – which then give way to other emotions as the reality of the situation sets in. We experience anticipation, apprehension, some fear, determination, and hope, to name a few. However, the driving motivations are to succeed and to be appreciated for what we bring to the group. The interesting thing is that what we bring to the group is interpreted and perceived in very different ways.

We react to our world as we encounter it. Our perception of reality and our understanding of it form expectations in our minds that are reflected in our behaviors. For example, as supervisors, we believe that we bring a wealth of knowledge, experience, and wisdom about how to accomplish the work. After all, we were one of the best. The expectations others have, however, usually relate to their position:

- The manager above you expects that you bring the skills to teach and provide guidance.
- The people who work for you hope you'll remove barriers and provide information that is useful.

Typically, expectations will be different from person to person, but that doesn't preclude that groups of people may have similar expectations due to common training or experience. In a group larger than five, however, the truth is that you probably will not be able to meet the expectations of every individual, let alone know what all the expectations are.

Expectations of groups are dynamic and, therefore, very difficult to meet from one point in time to another. The constantly changing expectations from the group, our perceptions about what we bring to the organization, and our current situation are all factors that drive certain behavior patterns. At first, these factors are a bit overwhelming to new supervisors, and their behavior reflects their inexperience. But as the supervisor gains confidence, we see that new behaviors are added that reinforce the supervisor's method and existence. There are a host of factors that drive behavior, but let's explore a common progression of traits exhibited by the 1st epiphany manager.

We Mimic What We Have Seen

One of the characteristics of human nature is that we tend to do as others around us have done, especially if it appears to have provided some success in a particular endeavor. This mimicking of behavior has worked well for us in the past. From living in caves and mimicking the behavior of successful hunters, we learned to hunt and find food. Those who didn't – well, they didn't survive. Mimicking is one of the basic human behaviors that defined survivors in our past as well as in our organizations today, and it is as necessary today as it was 10,000 years ago.

If you look at your own behavior, if you are successful, you probably found behaviors that, when you did the same thing, helped you achieve your goals. When I was learning to play golf, I mimicked the swing styles of Arnold Palmer, Jack Nicklaus, and Nick Faldo. I studied the commonalities and copied what they all did. It worked; I improved; and this success reinforced the behavior of mimicking for me.

At the beginning of our careers in management and leadership, we do the same thing. We watch and reflect the behavior of the leaders that we admire and want to be like. This is encouraged by the fact that most managers, when looking for someone to promote, look for someone who has the same traits that they have. In this way, people get a kind of double payback for mimicking the behaviors of their supervisors and leaders. They start to see what makes people successful and, at the same time, management is looking for those that are similar to themselves.

This phenomenon of mimicry is probably the reason for the old, Russian saying, "Meet the new boss, same as the old boss." From leadership change to leadership change, organizations that operate this way don't really change much at all, and people (workers, investors, etc.) shouldn't expect anything really new or different from the supposed changes. If they made great buggy whips in the past, they will make great buggy whips in the future, even though the market has left them behind.

So mimicking will lead to the same behavior as the last manager, good or bad. After all, what else do they have to go by? New managers who have only experienced the 1st epiphany will more often than not just follow in the footsteps of the last person that was in the position.

If it's not Broken, Don't Fix It

Many new managers have the perception that there is more than enough to fix and that anything that is perceived as working should not be disturbed lest they have to deal with it. Though this philosophy may never be stated, it can usually be seen in the manager's actions and behavior. They resist looking at new ideas and thrive on being the firefighter. They concentrate on fixing what is not working as designed instead of looking at better ways to do the tasks. Their language is often interlaced with words like "good enough" as they strive to meet the requirements. The unstated goal is to maintain the status quo, as long as it meets the requirements of the organization.

If you are dealing with company software that is over five generations old, still based in DOS or Windows 3.1, your CIO/CTO is probably a 1st epiphany manager. If your basic processes to accomplish routine tasks are more than 30 years old, you are in a 1st epiphany organization (or part of a historical re-creation, or should be). If the statement "If it was good enough for (fill in the blank), then it's good enough for us" is heard, then you are working for a 1st epiphany manager.

The driving force behind this behavior is that the 1st epiphany manager is too busy with other tasks to innovate or even create an environment where innovation can flourish. Their behavior and environment supports and encourages maintaining things exactly as they are. Change is threatening and destabilizing. It evokes conflict and requires leaving the familiar behind. After all, 1st epiphany managers have too much to do to deal with all this change.

Has to be Done a Certain Way, Usually My Way

Because the 1st epiphany manager *knows* the *correct* way to perform the task, they make requirements that tasks must be performed in a certain way. It will extend to almost every task in the group. Even in tasks where they have little or no experience, the 1st epiphany manager will often come up with a method and make it a requirement like the TPS reports in the movie *"Office Space."*

When you ask a 1st epiphany manager why things are done this way, a common answer is "They have always been done this way." There is usually no logic or reason for the methodology. It's just the preference of the manager, even in the face of a more logical or efficient way.

Telling People What to Do

Another defining characteristic of the 1st epiphany manager is that they tell people what to do rather than explain what needs to be accomplished. In all probability, 1st epiphany managers were hired for their technical aplomb and so they know how to accomplish the required tasks probably better than most.

Consequently, the 1st epiphany manager's day will be spent letting people know how to do it. They move about their spaces making sure that people are busy doing exactly what they told them to do. This occupies a lot of their time because they have to tell their people each step and how to do it. After all, they were one of the best at the tasks, and their way is obviously better than any other way.

The 1st Epiphany

New people in the organization see this as helpful advice and appreciate the one-on-one attention to learn their jobs, which is gratifying to the manager and reinforces the behavior. While the 1st epiphany manager becomes more convinced they are doing a good job, others in the organization become increasingly annoyed at having to do their tasks in the exact way their manager tells them. The workers learn quickly that if they take any initiative at all, it is rebuked as not being efficient, not in accordance with policy, or not the way that the company wants it. They are told, "We have approved this methodology only," "You're not a team player," and "Why can't you do it this way?"

This behavior occurs because the 1st epiphany manager ties their leadership skills and expectations directly to the output of the group. If they just had a group of themselves, they know they could do so much better – after all, they were one of the best.

Hovering

One step beyond telling people what to do, yet similar in nature, hovering is the constant watching or monitoring of employees as they accomplish tasks. It is driven by the need to make sure that things are going exactly as they should because the supervisor believes they can't trust the people in the group to do their tasks the right way (either the way they were told to do them or the way the supervisor would have done them). And again, while a new employee may see hovering as individual attention during training, anything more than 5 percent of their time will cause others to see it as a sign of distrust.

As the 1st epiphany manager hovers, they invariably catch people performing tasks differently than they have specifically instructed and see this as a sign that their hovering behavior is necessary. Finding any faults in the behaviors of others will be seen as validation – and faults will always be found.

Hovering takes a lot of time and requires constant effort on the part of the 1st epiphany manager. They keep records and are able to show that they caught so many errors that would have been made if they were not doing this. This behavior is even perceived as needed by their managers because of the numbers.

When the numbers indicate that a certain person is not performing as they had been, they receive more direct attention, which leads to conflict and causes the individual under scrutiny to go into fight-or-flight mode. But the 1st epiphany manager continues the scrutiny, feeling further justified by any sign that the individual isn't completing tasks as prescribed and may even begin to consider whether the individual is a good fit for the company.

Nothing Goes Out Until I Review/Inspect It

Armed with evidence that even constant supervision doesn't ensure that things are being done specifically the way the manager wants them to be done, the 1st epiphany manager typically moves to be the final inspection authority. This may satisfy their need to protect their reputation; but remembering that they were selected because of their above-average performance, the general output of the group would naturally be below the quality or quantity the manager would expect.

Upon initial inspection of the output of the group, the 1st epiphany manager is likely to find the quality or quantity is lacking and reports this. They build the justification for inspecting and reviewing all outputs. To their managers they appear to be improving the performance of the group; but while this is temporarily true, the group's performance will always suffer in other ways.

Whether it is emails, widgets, graphic presentations, or reports, the 1st epiphany manager must see, review, and approve the product. This will normally include fixing things with it. While occasional quality checks are to be expected, they continually try to put their own stamp on it, whether that is rephrasing a memo, modifying a part, or changing a presentation. Since in their minds the product represents them personally, it must live up to and match their expectations.

Taking Over the Task(s)

Firm in the belief that the only way to secure their reputation for high performance is to take matters into their own hands, 1st epiphany managers very often take over the task themselves. You can almost hear the phrase, "If you want it done right, you have to do it yourself."

As you can imagine, this requires that the 1st epiphany manager spend a lot of time at work to make sure things are done right and to meet the deadlines for the tasks. Typical comments from the 1st epiphany manager to their managers include: "I'm working on getting the group up to speed," "I'm having quality/quantity issues with the group," and "Jones (or any employee name) doesn't seem to get it." Another telltale phrase is "I can't seem to get them to understand ..." While these statements alone do not define a 1st epiphany manager, they can indicate that something may be affecting the manager's ability to manage the group, especially if these things are said repeatedly after several months in the position.

At this stage of the manager's development, they tell people what to do and not why or how it fits into the context of the situation. Telling a person what to do rarely, if ever, causes understanding. And apart from the fact that taking over the tasks further distances the group and creates a downward spiral in its effectiveness, it also prevents the manager from progressing on the journey of leadership.

Getting Things Done, Come Hell or High Water

In high-stress situations, we naturally rely on the methodologies and behaviors that have been most successful for us in the past. So when faced with a looming deadline, the 1st epiphany manager turns to the tried and true, moving heaven and earth to make their commitments – even if they have to do everything themselves.

While it is not uncommon for other managers and leaders to get into this situation, the 1st epiphany manager takes over the *critical* tasks in an effort to make the deadline. They will be in the process, doing the work, and everyone else will become a support worker to them. They will work all night, if required, ordering people to do the overtime to support them. As the pressure mounts, the manager starts to bark orders, assigning the more important tasks to those they trust and menial tasks to those less trusted. This stratifies the work environment, creating a more toxic and dysfunctional existence.

Hiring People Who are Exactly like Them, or as Close as Possible

When it comes time for the 1st epiphany manager to consider people to hire, they naturally gravitate to people that most resemble themselves, thinking they will be more successful. After all, if they have the same capabilities and values as the manager, they should fit into the culture better and cause fewer problems.

However, this is not the best course of action for the organization because it causes organizational stagnation and discourages innovation. Without diversity, organizations fail to grow and will most likely falter and fail in dynamic markets.

If you notice that the manager seems to hire people that have the same interests and even resemble the manager (all male, tall, mid-20s, etc.), it's a good sign you could be working for a 1st epiphany manager.

Promoting the Best Performers of Critical Tasks

The 1st epiphany manager usually has a list of tasks that they perceive as being critical to the performance of the group (and themselves). It may or may not be written down, but they know them. If you don't know what they are, just ask. They will usually be glad to tell you. People who can perform these tasks in the same manner in which the manager desires will be noticed and are likely to be promoted.

The 1st epiphany manager sees these people as great team players, people who *get it*, and examples of how others should behave. Remember that this is a direct reflection of the methodologies and philosophies of the manager. The manager will be excited if you can put the product of the manager and the employee next to each other and cannot tell the difference.

Conformity is of the utmost importance to the 1st epiphany manager, and by promoting the best performers of these critical tasks, it ensures that things will continue to be done their way while sending the message that conformity is highly valued in the group.

Promoting the best performers is not always best for the organization. When people move into supervision and management, the skill sets are very different, far different than those required to be individual contributors. First epiphany managers actually hurt organizations by promoting the best technical people and overlooking those who have the desire and aptitude for leadership.

Firing Those Who Don't Fit In

In their quest to eliminate non-conformity, a large amount of time is dedicated to monitoring those that don't fit in. People who behave, think, or look differently from them are all suspect. The 1st epiphany manager will spend more time with these people telling them exactly what needs to be done and documenting the mistakes that are inevitably found. This leads to more monitoring (hovering) and increasingly more specific instructions to the person. The cycle builds until both are so frustrated that the employee either quits or is fired for not performing to expectations.

Everything will be properly documented – the additional time spent with the person, the errors/mistakes (which will be more than others in the group), and the person's actions or responses (usually very negative) to the increased assistance. From the perspective of the legal department, the manager did everything possible to prevent a lawsuit. In the eyes of the human resources department, the policies and procedures were followed. In reality, the organization lost a valuable, innovative, and productive employee.

Sometimes leaders must eliminate those who don't perform or who by their own actions require removal from the organization. The key difference in the process outlined above is that conformity of behavior is used as reason to eliminate the person. By contrast, if you were to visit Google, you would see a group of people that seem to have nothing in common and use very different methods to obtain the goals of the company. The 1st epiphany manager values conformity to their likeness; but the real value to the organization lies in people's differences, methods, and varying perspectives.

There are a lot of examples of those who were fired or not hired because they didn't fit in: Walt Disney, Soichiro Honda, Thomas Edison, Albert Einstein, and Elvis Presley, to name a few. Unfortunately, in the pursuit of conformity, the 1st epiphany manager consistently overlooks the true value of the people in their group that are different.

The 1st Epiphany Manager's Meeting

It is surprising to realize that the same individual given the same circumstances can behave so differently having reached each of the epiphanies, but that is quite literally the case. Once an epiphany takes hold in an individual, it is hard to operate as before. And so in each of the chapters that describe the epiphanies, The Meeting is an opportunity to observe the manager in action and to demonstrate the different results that come from the manager's new behavior.

Having examined some of the most prevalent behaviors of 1st epiphany managers, let us look at how a hypothetical meeting held by this type of manager might proceed.

Background & Setting: In an automotive parts manufacturing company employing over a thousand people, a mandatory meeting to discuss new safety requirements is scheduled. Notice of the meeting and a copy of the new safety requirements were sent out by management to the group of eight people a week before the meeting. The new safety requirements are to be implemented no later than four weeks from the meeting date. The meeting is to be held in a meeting room off the factory floor at the start of the shift, 8:00 a.m. The manager is the first-level supervisor.

Manager:	(Arriving 10 minutes late to ensure that everyone is there so they don't have to repeat themselves to those who miss it – again.)
	Everyone got the memo in their mail boxes, so I'll get right to the point. We need to increase our eye protection in the Machine 14 area; and since that is our area, I'm requiring that all people on my shift now must wear safety glasses. I took the time to order some and I have them here. Pick up one pair from the box and sign the roster page next to your name stating that you received your pair.
Worker 1:	What about those of us who wear glasses already?
Manager:	I ordered the type that will fit over glasses. Make sure that you get yours; I'm making it a requirement that you wear them all the time now. If you don't, then there will be disciplinary action. Any other questions?
Workers:	(Silence.)
Manager:	Good. Everyone will be required to wear safety glasses by start of shift tomorrow. Pick up your glasses and sign the sheet stating that you received yours as you leave. I'll check the list to see that everyone signed.
Workers:	(Everyone picks up their glasses, signs the roster page, and shuffles out.)

These behaviors may seem extreme, but if you are a leader of a group or organization, at one time in your life you were the example of a 1st epiphany manager. You may have grown quickly through the stage, but to some degree you acted in this fashion for at least a little while. It's part of a journey that we all must make as leaders. And any of us can and will act in the behaviors presented if the circumstances dictate it, even 4th epiphany leaders.

Behaviors in 1st Epiphany-Managed Organizations

Newton's third law of motion tells us that for every action, there is an equal and opposite reaction. This law of action and reaction applies to organizations as well, although not quite as precisely. Every action by the leader will have an effect on the organization; but because reactions in an organization depend on a multitude of factors – many more than in the classical physics view of the world – the sheer number of variables prevents us from accurately predicting any one individual's behavior. We can use statistical analysis and sociology to predict how a hundred people are likely to react in response to a leader's actions, but we cannot predict how any one person will react.

So recalling the behaviors we observe in 1st epiphany managers, we can begin to predict the reactive behaviors that organizations are likely to experience. Your organization or group may reflect all or some of the following behaviors:

Check in to Work; Check out of Reality

Is the general attitude to put in your eight hours and get out as quickly as possible? Is the suggestion box empty? Do all the ideas come from managers?

First-epiphany-managed organizations often experience the situation where people come to work and hang up their brains at the door. No one ever makes suggestions or comes up with ideas at work – other than how to get time off. These are all indications that the organization has a 1st epiphany manager.

Because this type of manager has actually substituted their perception of how things should work instead of living in reality, any questions or issues are always solved in the manager's context. Likewise, the manager creates an environment where anything that mimics or comes from the manager is appreciated and anything that doesn't is shunned or, worse, completely ignored.

When managers set up this type of environment, they ignore the employees and the employees respond by ignoring everything except that which will keep them employed. In short, they *check out*.

Do Just What Needs to Be Done

In response to the 1st epiphany manager's micromanagement of the group – the hovering, telling people what to do, the constant control of the output – the group adapts and soon realizes that it is more efficient to wait and be told what to do than to venture out and undertake the tasks themselves. With the manager involved in virtually every aspect of the group, proactive behavior ceases to exist and people simply wait around until the manager assigns the specific tasks. A great deal of time is wasted waiting for others to accomplish their tasks and, in general, inefficiency starts to rise.

With management telling people things such as "Pick up the box and move it to the designated spot," employees do exactly that and then wait at that location for further orders. By some definitions, the actions of the employees can even be considered malicious compliance – doing exactly what they are told to do whether they believe it is the right thing or not.

No one expends extra effort or volunteers for overtime. At this point, the environment the 1st epiphany manager has created becomes so untenable that even the enticement of additional pay is negated. People just put in their 40 hours and they are out of there.

Cubicle Withdrawal

First epiphany managers are everywhere, and so are the strategies employees use to deal with them. One of the most common is seen in offices where the workers withdraw to their cubicles, put their heads down, and get through the eight hours with as little contact from the manager as possible. Though exaggerated for effect, the movie *"Office Space"* cleverly portrayed the environment created by the 1st epiphany manager and the classic withdrawal behavior of the workers to their cubicles. Blue collar workers, white collar workers, and professionals can all come under the oppression of this type of manager, though, and whether the retreat is to a cubicle, an office, break room, or roof, the reaction is the same.

When you find a company where the employees are dug into their cubicles with very little interaction, you might start observing the behavior of the managers to see if they are the cause. More often than not, you will find that they are.

Complaints to Human Resources (HR)

A 1st epiphany manager will have more complaints to HR than any other style of manager. Complaints will be about unfairness, favoritism, sexual harassment, and over management policies and rules.

The real reason the 1st epiphany manager draws so many complaints is because they don't listen to their employees. With no means to address their concerns, employees go to the only place they believe they will be heard within the organization, which is HR. However, most complaints will not be found to be actionable since they stem from a perception that the manager is simply ignoring the wishes and concerns of the employees. And it is likely that the manager will be found to have addressed the concerns (especially those that the manager equates to the group's performance) but never gave feedback or response to the employees.

Putting In For Transfer Becomes a Hobby

As most people cannot afford to lose their source of income, they do the next best thing – put in for a transfer. This is the fight-or-flight reaction to conflict in practice. When employees cannot fight with the manager (i.e., it becomes unproductive or career-limiting), they "take flight" via transfers.

HR usually spots this activity and will inquire; but unless there is some illegal or other litigious reason for it, normally no action will occur. The entire situation may present to HR as a confusing series of events that don't necessarily rise to the level where HR can take action. And since 1st epiphany managers hire others that resemble themselves, it is possible that HR may suffer from the affliction as well, so be wary of organizations that have a lot of transfers and moves.

Increased Sick Time

While not a definitive trait of the 1st epiphany manager's group, it could indicate there is a problem. HR usually provides reports of sick and off time to the management staff for evaluation and action. If the group is having more sick time than other similar groups or maxing out the sick-time quotas, it could be that a 1st epiphany management style is to blame.

Looking For New Opportunities

After a few months in the 1st epiphany manager's group, most people will start actively looking for new opportunities. In addition to transfers, they will contact other companies and organizations looking for a new position. Discussions at lunch will turn to who's hiring, how to update a resume, and networking. Looking for a new job can become a full-time occupation for some.

High turnover is almost a definitive indication of a 1st epiphany-managed organization. But when asked to account for the high turnover in their group, the 1st epiphany manager will first explain it as clearing out the "deadwood" or making room for those that will fit into the new culture.

Unionization

Whenever I have seen unionization occur, it has always been because of the actions of management. The most common reason is that no one in management takes the time to communicate to the employees and understand their issues. When people elect to unionize, it's a cry to be heard and appreciated – and in some cases respected. In my experience, unionization doesn't necessarily benefit the workers financially; in fact, in the instances with which I am familiar, the results were financially detrimental to the workforce. But the profound lack of appreciation from management was so compelling that fiscal concerns played a minimal role in their decision.

In an organization where unionization is occurring, it is probably because there are many 1st epiphany managers in it who, because they live in their own reality, disregard anybody else's perspectives as irrelevant or simply not true.

Working in a 1st-epiphany-managed situation is not fun. It is a dictatorial environment with harsh consequences for not conforming to the expectations of the manager. Increased monitoring and micromanagement is to be expected, and earning trust will be next to impossible. The general morale of the group is very low and many people exist in fight-or-flight mode.

The good news is that, with any luck, the manager will mature in place and things will get better. The other good news is that, in my estimation, only about 5 to 10 percent of mangers get stuck in this category. While we all pass through the phase, some fail to experience the next epiphany. Sometimes the 1st epiphany phase only lasts a couple of months; sometimes it lasts forever.

Working for a 1st Epiphany Manager

So you have landed in one of these situations. What can you do to help yourself and the manager? Well, the answer to that question is … it depends. In psychology, there are very few definitive answers and, therefore, few definitive actions to take. For the most part, 1st epiphany managers that are new to management can be molded and trained. In fact, they actually crave this advice and training. The catch is that they may only be receptive to this advice and training from very specific sources that they perceive as knowledgeable and experienced.

If you have a good deal of experience in the area being managed, you may have an advantage. Psychologists call this positional power. Because of your position, the new manager may give you automatic deference. I say this with some caution. People that have been in positions for many years may be seen as inferior due to not being promoted or lacking the right attitude to succeed. It is important to find out the manager's perception of you before you attempt these suggestions.

For those that have stayed at the 1st epiphany level for years, it will be very difficult, if not impossible, to get them to see their world differently. Their management style has long since adapted to their organizational setting and been proven successful, reinforcing the belief in their method. The only options in this situation are to learn to exist within the organization or leave, because advocating change will not be seen with favor.

Even so, please don't equate age or years in position as the only guidance for whether a person can change. Changing one's personal values and culture can happen at any age and situation. It can happen gradually or occur overnight; it can come easily or be harder than it has to be. My advice is to try some of the following behaviors and, if they work, then you and the manager have made progress.

Expect a Learning Curve

With any new manager, whether new to managing or just to your group, you should expect a learning curve. The person new to managing may feel that they are drinking from a fire hose and have a great many insecurities about their capabilities. Even an experienced manager will have a steep learning curve getting to know all the people of their group, as well as each of their strengths and weaknesses.

Recognizing that this is just a phase that all new managers go through, it is best to simply exercise a little tolerance and position yourself as a reliable member of the group. At first, the new manager's methods may seem unpredictable as they decide how best to approach their new situation. But as the manager adapts and settles into a more predictable routine, you may then be able to implement some of the suggestions that follow as they relate to the traits your manager is exhibiting.

Earn Respect

With this manager, it doesn't matter if you have been doing the same job for over 20 years, you will have to earn their respect. This is a new person with a new perspective on you and your work. And the best way to earn respect is to find out what their performance expectations are and meet or exceed them. This will not be easy as it is likely that they have a record of high performance, a very high set of expectations, and lofty goals for their new position.

In this case, the best advice might be to under-promise and over-deliver. But be careful not to leave the impression that you are sandbagging just to make your numbers. Your output will have to be as good as theirs used to be, or at least what they perceived it to be.

Another trait that will earn respect is if your manager can come to expect that you will always tell the truth and won't sugarcoat things. They usually don't have the time to deal with trying to decipher anything else.

Saving Face

All people are slaves to some social norms. The trick is figuring out which norms we are talking about. We are social creatures by nature and have an innate desire to find our place in society. Again, this is the society of our choosing and may not reflect the mainstream of the population, or any population for that matter.

Saving face is an important social norm for many Asian cultures and a defining characteristic for all 1st epiphany managers. And just as it would be important for a businessperson working in Japan, for instance, to respect this aspect of Asian culture, it is also critical never to underestimate the importance of saving face to the 1st epiphany manager.

The manager's self-image is tied to how people perceive them, which may seem paradoxical since they don't appear to care what other people think of them at all. But the reality is that they care very much what *certain* people think of them, principally, their manager.

So with this in mind, it may be possible to garner some credibility and respect from your manager if your actions are supportive of your manager's goals to save face. An example of this may be publicly supporting one of their policies or other actions that you deem worthy of support. (I wouldn't recommend that you support actions that you do not with good conscience support yourself. Few are more scorned in organizations than hypocrites.)

Another way to help the manager save face is to tell them privately when you think they have done a good job. With this manager and the sociological environment of his group, this is better done in private lest others see it as an attempt to grasp favoritism.

Ask What the Expectation Is – Make Sure You Can Meet It

There are expectations around every task that relate to time and quality. And while new managers are usually quite capable of telling their group what tasks to do and how to do them, they often fail to discuss any of the other expectations that provide context to the person doing the work.

New managers are typically not experienced in putting expectations in language or meaning that is pertinent to the person doing the work. For instance, a producer may tell a worker to create an article about dogs at the park but fail to mention that the article is needed in two hours and is simply meant as filler material which should only be 200 words long. Without information about the expectations, the writer may leave to do research at the park thinking they need to write a lengthy lead article.

In many cases, you will have to help the manager put the expectations in terms that you can control and meet. So when the manager says that you need to increase production, you might clarify that each person should then be producing ten more widgets per hour, something they can track themselves. If you know you cannot meet the expectation, then you need to ask for help to resolve the difficulty. Clarifying expectations helps ensure that you are working effectively to meet the goals of your manager, but it also helps the manager gain more experience dealing with people and learning to speak their language – and those are skills that help them progress on their journey of learning leadership.

Keep Communications Open, Even If It Appears Not To Be Appreciated

First epiphany managers strive to do a good job. It's just that they may not have the skills yet to do a great job. One of the primary tasks of the new manager is to ensure communications are open and working well. Help out the manager in meetings by providing important information to the group and the manager. Keep the lines of communication open even if the manager doesn't seem to appreciate it.

Providing valuable information about the status of the work or obstacles will help the manager and group deal with reality. Being the person that knows and promulgates important, timely information can help you earn respect and trust as well.

Train Your Boss – Offer Suggestions and Advice Privately

When things are not going well, make a suggestion or provide advice in a private setting, remembering that you have to help them save face. This advice needs to be of a non-personal nature, such as, "I'd like to recommend that we move the meeting to 3:00 p.m. so that we address all shifts at shift turnover." If you give advice that is personal in nature, "You really should speak louder to the group," that would come across as a specific attack on the person. Regardless of the intention or how the person reacts, if it's personal, it will be regarded as an attack. Stay away from personal advice with this level of manager.

Another technique in this train-your-boss topic is to invite your boss to watch you perform your job, especially if they are inexperienced in the area. By showing your new 1st epiphany manager what you do and your level of expertise in the area, they can use you as a resource. It's important to offer suggestions and advice carefully, however, because a person will only learn if they have the need or desire to learn.

Ask For Clarification

Asking for clarification is tricky as it can be seen from different perspectives, such as, the person asking is not quick enough to catch on, not paying attention, or just being annoying. On the other hand, it can be construed as being interested, being concerned, or possibly the person being perceived as the natural leader of the group.

So when do you ask for clarification with the 1st epiphany manager? My recommendation is to ask when the topic is of passionate interest to the manager or when you believe that the manager could teach something worthwhile to the group as a whole.

When we deal with 1st epiphany managers, we need to understand that, for most, they are on a journey to becoming a great leader. This is just the first part of that journey and, as with any journey, they learn as they go along. Helping the manager become a great leader is a truly rewarding activity in life. Just like rearing your own child, the journey is not always fun and will have its moments, but the results can sometimes be spectacular. To help a person along this path, what you are doing is actually changing the environment so that the person can see a reality that is not what they thought it was. You are setting up the opportunity to have the next epiphany.

Pathways to the 2nd Epiphany

If you have read this chapter and see some of the behaviors in your own actions and your group shows some of the reflective behaviors, then you have to realize that you are probably operating at the level of a 1st epiphany manager. While this may not be your entire modus operandi, remember back to when there was a lot of stress in a situation. How did you deal with it? What actions did you take? Are they reflective of 1st epiphany management?

During times of stress, we usually fall back on what has worked for us in the past. We go back to basics, as it were. Actions are telltales of what our true beliefs and values are. They reflect where we truly are in our journey to be great leaders.

One of the paradoxes in human psychology is that people's behaviors reflect their internal values and beliefs. But it is also true that if a person acts differently and finds it to be successful, the new actions will drive a change of the internal values. It appears that if you act differently, you start to think differently, and that changes your internal values and beliefs. So how do you effect change? You change by changing your behavior.

Changing your behavior works for most lightly held values and beliefs. As an example, changing from taking your car to work to taking the train in all likelihood will give you a different perspective about commuting. You might even change your work habits and enjoy the commuting time. This is an example of a lightly held value. You may have exchanged the value of flexibility for extra stress-free personal time on the train. For deeply held beliefs or values, this technique will not work. As an example, starting to celebrate Christmas and Easter will not make you Christian any more than wearing a kippah will make you Jewish.

For new 1st epiphany managers, most all of the values and beliefs that drive behavior for this area are lightly held. If you have been a manager for a very long time, they will be more tightly held but still can be changed as the organization reflects different behaviors and you get different results.

People and organizations are all different, and not all of the techniques for change will work with all situations. The key is to try different things. This opens the opportunity to witness different reactions and to assess the effectiveness of the changes in your behavior. Note that if you try something once and you get no reaction – which is normal – as the saying goes, "Try, try again." Sustained effort over a period of time is necessary for changes to take hold, so be persistent.

As with any endeavor, change involves risk. You took on risk to be promoted, to do something different from what you were used to. Changing your behavior introduces some risk as well, although probably not as much as you imagine. When we work with organizations, we deal with people. For the most part these people want to be successful and appreciated for what they do and provide to the group. So if you think about it, they have just as much at stake as you do in these changes. They want you to succeed as their leader/manager as much as you do.

Earlier, I discussed the process of change. One of the requirements of change is to observe something that makes you think and evaluate your behaviors (expressions of your values and beliefs). You can actually initiate this process by trying different behaviors, and the organization or group will reflect your new behavior. If you want to see how this works, just try coming to work two hours earlier each day and see what kind of reactions you get. The organization will react. I'm not sure exactly how it will react in your specific situation, but I guarantee that it will react.

If you determine that you have a tendency to act as a 1st epiphany manager, the following suggestions can help you create situations where you can learn from and hopefully experience new realizations about people, organizations, and yourself.

Find a Mentor

A mentor is a wise and trusted counselor, someone that is more experienced and knowledgeable who is willing to give their time and insight to support your growth. They encourage their mentees by providing learning experiences and dialogue, challenging unproductive habits and sparking new thoughts. They are someone in whom you can confide, ask for honest feedback (and get it), and who will make themselves available to you (most of the time anyway). A mentor and mentee choose each other. They should not be assigned by some upper level manager or committee. They might work at the same company or they might not. They could be a member of your faith, service club, or other organization.

Don't pick a mentor that is just like you. If doing the same thing over and over and expecting different results is the definition of insanity, then picking a mentor that is just like you would be the perfect example of it. Diversity is the key to personal and professional growth and, if you think back on the people you learned the most from, odds are they held very different perspectives about life than you and weren't like you at all.

Instead, choose a mentor that has a natural following. Look for someone who can get groups of people to be inspired and accomplish great things. You can find them by their works and their inspired followers. Skip ahead and familiarize yourself with the characteristics of a 4th epiphany leader's organization and evaluate that leader as a possible mentor.

It takes courage to ask someone to be your mentor. It's a self-proclamation that you need to learn and an affirmation that you're willing to do what it takes to grow. When you do ask someone to be your mentor, make sure that they have the time to dedicate. Being a true mentor can be a lifetime endeavor and have lifetime rewards for both involved. Most 4th epiphany leaders will make the time because helping tomorrow's leaders is one of their passions.

I could probably write a book on mentoring, but here are a few key aspects to help you make the process more successful.

- *Set regular meetings.*

Weekly meetings are helpful at first, but then monthly meetings work best after the first month or two. For this process to work, you both need to spend time together – so be respectful and fit into your mentor's schedule. Remember that you asked them for help, so be the one that makes the effort. Most 4th epiphany leaders will make the time as they understand how important it is to mentor someone.

- *Be brutally honest.*

Lying to your mentor is the same as lying to yourself. They cannot help you if they don't understand your true situation. Mentors will be open and honest with you about their experiences and recommendations. While there is no legal protection for what is said confidentially, be as forthcoming as possible. Don't talk about inside company information, but rather how your actions are being received and whether they are effective or not. Don't make what you discuss a liability for both you and your mentor.

- *Keep commitments.*

During the mentoring process, your mentor will probably give you things to do or investigate. When you make a commitment to do this, make sure that you follow through. Failing to keep a commitment to your mentor is a sure way to get them to question your commitment to the process. On the other hand, keeping your commitments shows that you appreciate what your mentor is doing for you and will strengthen the relationship.

> *"Those who cannot change their minds cannot change anything."*
>
> *George Bernard Shaw*

Be prepared to explore new perspectives. It is the mentor's job to get you to consider different opinions, possibilities, and methods. And it is up to you to keep an open mind. When you agree to be mentored, you are committing to take your own road less traveled knowing that growth only happens when we are willing to change our minds and take a different path. And on this journey, it is wise to be like an innocent child that is fond of asking the big questions of "Why?" Learn the why of your mentor's opinions, actions, and reasoning. Mentoring is the act of leading a person along a path of discovery. Make sure that your eyes (and mind) are open.

Learn To Trust People

When people show up for their first day of work, they have great attitudes and want to do their best. They want to succeed and be appreciated. They come to work trusting that their managers have assigned them meaningful work that if done skillfully, quickly, or artfully will be appreciated. Managers expect that the people who work for them will use the resources provided to them in an effective and efficient manner. For both of these things to happen, the employees must trust the management and management must trust the employees. If an atmosphere of trust is not present, then the processes become inefficient and wasteful.

When I investigate organizations that don't work efficiently, I usually find that the issue is a matter of trust or, rather, the lack of trust. It brings to my mind the Spaghetti western *"The Good, The Bad And The Ugly"* where Clint Eastwood, Lee Van Cleef, and Eli Wallach each have a gun pointed at the other in the classic standoff situation. The tension mounts until someone fires and the hail of bullets inevitably reveals its destruction. But, of course, that is how standoffs are resolved in Spaghetti westerns. In business, tensions mount as well but the resolution can end less dramatically if someone lowers their gun and starts a dialogue.

If you are a manager where the relations between management and employees are tense, you can choose to continue to "hold the gun" or make a move to better the situation.

Someone has to lower their gun first, and it should be you. Learn to trust your people. After all, they didn't start off wanting to make mistakes and be difficult. They had good attitudes and intentions at one time. Try to create an environment of trust and mutual appreciation again. The first step of this is to find some way to convey trust.

For each person that works for you, find some way to trust them. Assign a task and inspect the product, not the process. Does it meet your expectations? Did they accomplish what you needed to have done? If they have, give them the appreciation that they deserve. Sometimes a simple "thank you" is all they need. A "good job" now and then goes a long way. Try it. You might be surprised at the results.

You probably will not change attitudes or behaviors overnight, or even over the next month for that matter, but be persistent. Some organizations have been distrusting each other for so long that it has become a way of life for them. Keep at it; you are making progress one person at a time, even if it doesn't show right away.

Delegate ... Really

On the topic of trust comes delegation. Delegation is the act of entrusting, assigning or transferring authority or commission. In the truest sense of the word, you are appointing a person as your representative. This sounds a lot different from telling people what to do, doesn't it? There have been hundreds of books written on the topic of delegation, but they all boil down to trust. You trust that they will do the task as you would have, and they trust that you have given them the tools and information to be successful. You are giving a person the ability to act in your place, and with that they have your reputation.

It sounds scary to most of us that someone else can affect how others see us or regard our abilities. If your team performs well, then people say it's a reflection of the leadership; and if you are the leader, that's personal. We are held responsible for the outcomes of our group.

The fact is that we cannot do it all ourselves and we have to delegate the work. If we assume that the person wants to do a good job, we are clear on our expectations of the outcome, and provide the resources necessary to accomplish the task within the time allowed, there should be success. The first step is to believe that people want to do a good job. This is the part where you must take the initiative to trust first. In organizations that have historically displayed their lack of trust in their relationships, this may take several attempts to be successful. But continue on. Work with your mentor to help you learn techniques to improve the chances of success.

Be proactive and read books on delegation. Practice with your mentor. It's not as easy as I have outlined it here and it will require practice. The difficulties come from the needs of each employee. While the basics of delegation are the same for all, the way you implement things will be different for each. What works for some won't work for others. In delegation, you truly are leading the organization one person at a time. Don't give up. Keep working to improve and get improving results. Remember that for both you and your delegate, you are both learning how to work with each other. It will take time.

Ask "How Would You Do It?"

Did you ever think what it means to a person to ask them "How would you do it?" From the perspective of the person being asked, it is an affirmation that they are valued, that what they think and say are worthwhile to hear and understand. It is a form of appreciation. Appreciation is one of the truly universal motivators for people. If you can show people that you appreciate them, they will reflect that with respect and trust.

Asking for input on a particular situation or problem gets people involved. Most of the time they have different perspectives that can enlighten the group, which moves the group closer to a solution. What you are trying to do is engage all the brain power in your group. The people that you have working for you also have experience, knowledge, and skills that can solve problems too. They do it every day. Why not let them apply that resource to the problems that you have in the group? Besides, you just may be surprised at what they come up with.

With this technique, again, you have to be persistent. Just asking the question once in a meeting and getting no response could show you that your group has been oppressed for some time. When you do get an answer, no matter how much you think it absurd, ask others what they think of it. While you may make the final decisions, don't squelch the dialogue before it gets started. Allow it to proceed and see if it gets you headed in the right direction. Intervene only when the conversation starts to go astray. Guiding a meeting and getting everyone involved takes practice. Your mentor can help you learn and practice the technique.

What do you do if you consistently do not receive any answers? Keep at it. What do you do when you get a good solution? Praise and thank the person in front of the group. This will encourage others to participate. Some of the best solutions to problems that I have faced came from others. I'm sure that if you keep asking, some of your best solutions will come from other people too.

If you follow the advice and actions in this section, you should start to see opportunities to experience group dynamics in ways that you may not have thought possible in the past. This is only the start of your journey, and there is much more to learn and do. As you and the group grow (yes, groups mature only as fast as their leader), you will get to experience a type of synergy. The group will go through phases under your guidance. It will be a lot like learning any new skill. There will be times that you'll wonder if it is all worthwhile and times that you'll remember with great fondness your entire life. One thing I can promise is that it *is* worth it. Nothing is more worthy an endeavor than to be in the position to unite a group of people in a worthwhile cause and accomplish great things.

At this point in this journey, you should have a mentor and have started to learn the basics of delegation. You should be starting to understand the relationship between trust and group involvement. One of the most important lessons that you should start to understand is the power of appreciation – how you can learn to appreciate people and how they react in response to that appreciation.

Leadership is a learned skill. Some people come by it naturally, but most of us have to work at it. We need to learn and practice the skills to be great leaders; and in our learning, we must keep our minds open so that we can take in new ideas, recognize new realities, and change our behaviors. If you have read this far and have begun to implement the suggested actions, you have the capability to be a great leader.

"Learning to trust is one of life's most difficult tasks."

Isaac Watts

Chapter 3

The 2nd Epiphany

I was managing a group of skilled craftspeople in the late '90s. We needed to get some major maintenance done and, as luck would have it, I came down with the flu. I tried to stay in phone communication with the group; but, because of my condition, I was only able to outline a brief list of tasks that needed to be done. When I finally returned to work a week later, I found that the entire list had been accomplished. I immediately went out to check the work and to my delight (and relief) everything had been done perfectly, but I noticed that some of the supplies I set aside had not been used.

When I asked about the unused supplies, I learned that someone in the group had come up with a completely different way to accomplish the tasks which didn't require the supplies I had ordered. I naturally had my doubts as to the quality of the work; but upon inspection I saw that it not only met my expectations, it actually exceeded them. I asked how he had done the work and he showed me that he had built a rig which eliminated the need for the supplies and actually achieved a better result than the method I had imagined. I was at the beginning of my second epiphany.

The 2nd Epiphany:

It doesn't have to be done my way to meet the expectations.

I began to experiment. For a few in the group, I simply told them what the outcome needed to be and let them figure out how to get it done. To my surprise, in almost every instance, the jobs were done properly and usually exceeded my expectations. As you can imagine, I felt the weight being lifted off my shoulders. I didn't have to tell them what to do all the time and could just give them the job and check the results. This freed up a lot of my time. Wow.

Once I realized that it doesn't have to be done my way, it can be done Mark's way or Mary's way and still meet the expectations or requirements, I didn't have to spend the time to tell people how to do things anymore. The group seemed to enjoy this new style of management too. It was amazing to me that most of my people now seemed to *get it*, and were able to do a good job. Truth be known, it was about this time that I realized that the problems with the group could be traced back to me and my *management* style. You too could be making this realization.

Sometime after you start asking people "How would you do it?" you start to realize that you are getting some very good answers – and, if you're honest with yourself, some of the ideas are much better than yours. You start to recognize that there are people in the group who consistently come up with great ideas and means to accomplish the tasks. When you start to trust these people with the more important tasks, you find they reward your confidence and generally always meet your expectations.

The 2nd epiphany level is where I see most managers. In my very unscientific opinion, I estimate that about 40% of management has progressed to this point but never ventured beyond into true leadership – and there may be good reason. Many management and leadership courses teach old, outdated ideas which survive not because they are efficient, but because they *appear* to make sense and because very little work has been done to controvert them. For example, the idea that people need close supervision is not valid in most situations, and the philosophy that you need to maintain control is pure fallacy.

A lot of what is taught about management and leadership ignores basic human behavior, and that is its failing. And this is of great concern to me, as it reflects in the organizations that we lead. We saw that there is a great deal of waste in the 1st-epiphany-managed organization. The 2nd epiphany manager is learning to operate differently, but typically does not get the maximum benefit from their organization and this represents a very large resource that is not being used effectively. When I study 2nd-epiphany-managed organizations, I estimate that they leave 50 percent of the organization's human capability unused.

The 2nd epiphany manager is truly a manager. They are maintainers and firefighters, concerned with getting the processes to run smoothly and eliminating all the problems – as opposed to getting the maximum out of their people. Managers are needed and serve vital roles in organizations. But while these types of managers are necessary, this book is about leadership and the path to becoming a leader. Many people are happy and do well at this level, but moving beyond is the focus of this book.

In my studies of leadership and group psychology, there are very direct connections between the actions of leadership and the behavior, culture, and morale of the organization. You will start to realize this as you continue on your journey to becoming a leader. If your organization is performing well, it is because you have created an environment wherein they can succeed. If the organization is performing poorly, again, it is because you didn't make it so that they could succeed. More on this later, but for now let's see how just this one major epiphany changes the behavior of the manager and group.

Behavioral Traits of the 2nd Epiphany Manager

"Slow and steady wins the race."

Unknown

One of the most commonly held misperceptions about 2nd epiphany managers is that they trust people, but in reality trust is only skin deep at this level. They may have come to accept that other methods can effectively accomplish tasks, but their unstated goals often remain the same as when they were 1st epiphany managers. The 2nd epiphany manager is still usually very concerned with performance and maintaining their image in the workplace, even if they appear to have relaxed on exactly how that is accomplished. Instead of hovering and taking control of tasks themselves, though, the 2nd epiphany manager is likely to put faith in process as a means to control workflow and achieve high performance – and this produces the outward appearance of trust.

The ratio of trust to distrust is probably the same as the amount of an iceberg that you can see above water. Trust is the 10 percent that is visible. Whereas the 1st epiphany manager is all about keeping things the same, the 2nd epiphany manager focuses on just moving things at their pace – which is usually glacial in speed. You may hear a lot of discussion about great ideals, but when you look at the manager's actions, the real internal values are revealed.

"Trust, but Verify"

In describing the policy of nuclear non-proliferation between the United States and the USSR, President Ronald Reagan made good use of the old Russian maxim, "Trust, but verify." And so it is with the 2nd epiphany manager. While they may be learning that people can get things done, they continue to make sure that the product is up to par with their expectations. They differ from the 1st epiphany manager in that they only check the outputs occasionally, if you have earned their trust. But having substituted faith in the process for direct control over the workflow, they invest their time in improving process. They search for and build checkpoints into the process to satisfy their need to verify that things are proceeding properly. The focus is to get it right, avoid problems, and maintain smooth operations.

If this behavior were restricted only to customer products, that would be construed as good quality control. The problem comes when the 2nd epiphany manager applies this process of periodic checking to the people in the group. At best, periodic checking is a hit-and-miss, sort of shotgun approach to identifying errors. The reason is that there is normally no statistical controls or graphical analysis, no feedback to improve process, only the correction of errors. Another problem is that this behavior will extend to everything from checking emails sent to clients to work performed by other internal organizations.

Specific Limits of Action – Training Wheel

The 2nd epiphany manager works very well in historical union environments where focus is on the division of labor. All tasks have been specifically assigned to vertical silos. People have specific tasks and these interlock with others. The goals are outlined very clearly in these silos of responsibility, and the 2nd epiphany manager is the gatekeeper and monitor of what goes into his silo and what doesn't.

People are also siloed in their scope of authority and action. You may have heard people say, "That's not my job," but this manager would say, "That's not your job." They see it as disruptive to the flow of things when people start doing things that are not part of their jobs. After all, if people are just doing whatever they want, how do you get anything done? The attitude is that if you want to try something new, go home; we do work here.

Assignment of Leads

Since some people have distinguished themselves to the 2nd epiphany manager through their keen understanding of the job, gaining the manager's trust, they are usually put in the position of lead or trainer for the group. A lead in this organization is specifically assigned to do the same thing that the manager would do if they had the time – verify and make sure the process is going smoothly and without problems. They are assigned to fight problems as they occur.

The leads are chosen by how much they reflect the manager and their values (even how much they look like the manager in some cases, unfortunately). Their logic is that if you choose something that is familiar, you typically have fewer problems with it, a fallacy which they apply to people as well. We may find it easier to communicate with people who have a similar background as ours or a common basis for understanding, but it doesn't necessarily provide a very fertile ground for learning new things. Experiencing something outside of our perceived reality is the requirement that makes learning possible for humans. Since this manager is focused on keeping things under control, new concepts, processes, things, or people can upset the apple cart, as it were. Hence, they promote and team with people that have the same focus as they do.

Implementation of the Suggestion Box

The 2nd epiphany manager will probably implement the suggestion box. While it sounds like a great idea in principle, they actually have mixed feelings about it. Philosophically, the idea of listening to their employees sounds good, but they realize that evaluating and responding to suggestions will interrupt the flow of things and take time away from making sure that everything is going right. There typically is no real process to evaluate or feed back to the employees that make suggestions. Most of the time the manager just reads the suggestions and usually finds some reason why they cannot be implemented (been tried before, costs too much, no one to do it, etc.)

Remember that the goal of this manager is to keep things moving smoothly with the least amount of disruption. So in reality, suggestions that cause processes to be radically changed will be met with resistance. Small changes that do not require changes on the part of the manager usually will be accepted and tried. This will be touted as actively promoting change and progress. While I cannot argue that progress is being made, for this manager and their organization, it will be more like improving buggy whips as opposed to inventing the transistor.

"But what is it good for?"

(Engineer at Advanced Computing Systems Division of IBM, commenting on the microchip in 1968.)

Hypocrisy

I want to preface this section with a statement of belief: We are all hypocrites at some level. We tell our children to follow the rules, but exceed the speed limit on the way to their school. I also believe that we all want to be the best that we can be and be examples to others, but for whatever reason we fall short. That being said, the 2nd epiphany manager's behavior will also appear hypocritical.

They stand and talk about treating everyone with fairness and equality. But if you watch carefully, you will see that some people are treated more fairly than others. This has nothing to do with race, religion, or heritage, but rather the person's internal values and how closely they match that of the manager. It is reinforced by the employee's performance and how closely it resembles the manager's and how much respect the manager has for the performance of that employee. Realize that this behavior may be similar or even the same as other managers, but the motivation is different.

So if the behavior is similar, how do you tell what the motive is? If you're the manager, evaluate what is causing you to make the decision. Are you choosing the person that will do best for the organization or the one that will cause the fewest problems for you? By choosing this person, will it make your life easier or harder? (Trick question.) Truly innovative people rarely make a manager's life easier.

If you are not the manager, it is much harder to tell. Determining motivation is tough. One way is to ask the manager. If they say they were the best person, ask why. If the answer has to do with past performance, attention to detail, best scores, things that have to do with the current process, odds are that the motivation was to make things easier for the manager. If the answer was something that sounds like the person was selected to bring radical change, you're probably not dealing with a 2nd epiphany manager. To truly find out, ask about the changes they expect to see. If it is to improve the processes, you are back to the 2nd epiphany manager.

Inconsistent Praise and Condemnation

This level of manager has progressed from trusting no one to trusting a few. And this is where the expectations of the manager create a self-fulfilling prophecy, and it works this way:

The 2nd epiphany manager starts to notice a person that seems to perform at the level they expect – in fact, the person seems to perform at a level that exceeds the expectations of the manager. The manager starts to praise this high performer for the great job they are doing. And then the manager starts to compare this high-performing person's output with the output of others, who will not match up. Next, the manager will investigate why other people in the group can't do the same level of work. (But notice that the manager doesn't look at why this person can perform at this level in the first place.) The other members of the group are then subjected to comparison and *help* in the form of more supervision or making the great performer a lead so that they can supervise them.

But by removing the best performer from the group, the manager has reduced the capabilities of the group. So even though the manager believes they've done the right thing, the group's output has actually decreased, requiring more supervision of people who have now also been told, whether directly or indirectly, that they are not measuring up.

Meanwhile, the high performer receives training on how to train people, and the manager starts to believe that they have been saddled with a group of under-achievers with bad attitudes. The manager rewards their high performers with praise and tries to motivate their *marginal* employees with threats of job security and overtime. You can see where this goes in a hurry.

Third and 4th epiphany managers realize that people are different and each brings specific talents and skills. Not all people are good at one thing, but rather everyone is good at something and they understand how to capitalize on this diversity. Again, it goes back to focus. Second epiphany managers are tuned in to process, not people. It may sound harsh; but in the 2nd epiphany manager's estimation, people are but cogs in the machine to be fixed or repaired.

Appraisals Held Once A Year, If That

It's not that the 2nd epiphany manager doesn't like to do appraisals or believes they are unnecessary; it's that appraisals interrupt the flow of things. The attitude is, "We have to stop what we are doing to get these done."

If you have an appraisal with a 2nd epiphany manager, it will be quick and efficient. More often than not, most people in the group will be rated better than average. This minimizes conflict and keeps things running smoothly. What's better than everyone getting above average? Doesn't it reflect the good job the manager has been doing managing and training the group?

Feedback will be noted and duly documented. Then it's back to work and "glad that's done" until next year.

Focus On Maintaining Steady, Controllable Improvement

Rapid improvement resembles something akin to chaos, which is threatening to the 2nd epiphany manager's sensibilities. Whereas they might acknowledge the need for constant improvement, they actively work to avoid it because it disrupts the smooth process they prefer. "How can you perfect the process if you keep changing it?" they ask. The easiest changes to make in this organization are things that don't affect the manager or disturb the even-keel environment they require. Slow and steady is the dogma promoted by this level of manager.

Focus On Keeping Things under Control

When you ask a 2nd epiphany manager to take a direction that they haven't had a chance to evaluate fully, you will more than likely get "I'll have to look at that first." That's because this level of manager is the most prone to paralysis by analysis. They want to understand how a decision will affect their operations in the minutest detail, lest something happens that they didn't anticipate.

In fact, with the 2nd epiphany manager, keeping things under control is more than mere desire, it is their defining characteristic. If you look at their behavior, you begin to see that most everything they do is focused on controlling their world.

In the name of keeping things under control, they limit the number of people they assign things to, trusting a few and monitoring the rest. When they are with peers, their discussions revolve around how to solve problems that have come up with their processes because they are almost completely process-oriented.

Training Is a Necessary Evil

If appraisals interfere with the normal flow of things, training interferes just as much. But since the 2nd epiphany manager sees that training is beneficial to some degree, it is tolerated. Training is also used to reward those whom the manager sees as top performers. Who best to send to training than those who can learn the fastest? These people are sent to training under the proviso that they will acquire skills and knowledge and then return to train others. But typically, time is never made for those who attended training to train the others because it disrupts the normal flow of operations.

Seems To Hate Meetings, but Goes To a Lot of Them

Like training, attending meetings is a necessary evil for the 2nd epiphany manager. They don't like meetings, but they attend a lot of them in order to find out what others are doing that could affect their operation. The information they learn at meetings helps them minimize the impact of any changes. Their purpose is to prevent changes and maintain the status quo.

In meetings, they will ask, "Why are we doing this?" and generally are the ones that bring up the reasons why things can't be done rather than how to get them done. They typically take very detailed notes. They like documentation to verify that things are not going to affect them or to recall specifically what they have agreed to do. Don't look for radical suggestions or new ideas from this manager in meetings, even when directly asked. If they send someone to a meeting for them, the instructions will be "Just take notes and don't agree to anything without calling me first."

Conflict Avoidance, the Peacemaker

When it comes to conflict, this manager will become the peacemaker, the king (or queen) of compromise. They don't like conflict and take whatever steps are necessary to avoid it because conflict creates problems and problems are to be avoided. They refer to union contracts, policy manuals, or other processes to adjudicate conflict. They like having processes for everything and that even includes how to deal with people. In their value system, people who cause conflict need to be *fixed* or *dealt with*, which is simply code for removing them from the group.

For the 2nd epiphany manager, dealing with emotional people is scary. People who cannot contain their emotions are obviously broken and need fixing. They prefer to let the HR department handle their people issues. After all, isn't that their job? Here again, the 2nd epiphany manager reinforces the practice of keeping silos of discrete work and responsibilities.

Conflict can occur in different groups as well. If there is conflict with a peer, for instance, the 2nd epiphany manager normally takes a few minutes to understand and clarify the issues with the peer before suggesting they take the matter up with their manager. For the 2nd epiphany manager, the end goal in this situation is to minimize the impact to their operation.

If the issue is with their manager, however, things can get very interesting from a psychological point of view. Second epiphany managers normally follow rules and appreciate a structured environment, so they will work hard to avoid any type of conflict with their manager. If, on the other hand, their manager is a 3rd or 4th epiphany leader, there might not be any rules or structure for this manager to work within – and this makes them feel quite uncomfortable. At some point they will either leave or make their own rules and structure.

Ordinarily, conflict with their manager will almost never take place; but when issues develop that make conflict unavoidable and it's in their face every day, the 2nd epiphany manager will capitulate and go back to their area ready to either surreptitiously ignore the issue as long as they can or make plans to leave.

Quick Caveat: If the 2nd epiphany manager is managed by a 2nd epiphany manager, it is likely that they will go around their manager to gain the favor and support of their manager's manager.

As you can see, the 2nd epiphany manager's entire focus is to maintain smooth, no-conflict operations. Therefore, things change slowly if at all, and they like it that way. If you are looking for someone to maintain an operation or process that requires little or no change for the foreseeable future, then the 2nd epiphany manager will make a great addition to your team, and in my experience, there are many organizations where this type of manager can thrive.

But before you select this type of person for your organization, you should consider if your operations need to keep up with the latest technology, operate in a competitive market, or constantly improve at a quick pace. If the answer is yes to any of these questions, it would be better to search for a manager or leader who has progressed further in the journey to leadership.

The 2nd Epiphany Manager's Meeting

The majority of the managers I have known are in this part of their journey. The normal 2nd epiphany manager is usually successful; and their organizations are, for the most part, successful in achieving their overall goals. Whereas this manager has learned to use the resources they have to get things done, they are primarily interested in maintaining their current performance and only react to outside pressures to change.

As in the section about 1st epiphany managers, The Meeting lets us watch the 2nd epiphany manager in action so we can see how this manager handles the exact same meeting situation.

Same Background & Setting: In an automotive parts manufacturing company employing over a thousand people, a mandatory meeting to discuss new safety requirements is scheduled. Notice of the meeting and a copy of the new safety requirements were sent out by management to the group of eight people a week before the meeting. The new safety requirements are to be implemented no later than four weeks from the meeting date. The meeting is to be held in a meeting room off the factory floor at the start of the shift, 8:00 a.m. The manager is the first-level supervisor.

Manager: (Arriving about 5 minutes early to see who can follow directions and who can't, the manager starts the meeting right on time, not waiting for those that can't seem to get it right.)

                I gave the memo to Bob to put in everyone's mailbox. The memo outlines our need to make sure that we are meeting the new safety requirements. The other thing in the memo is that we need to have all of our actions done, documented, and returned to the Safety Department within the next four weeks. When I read the memo, I believe that the only part that pertains to us is about the eye protection.

                Rick, the day shift lead, was given the task to identify where we need to address this issue in our operations. Rick identified, and I concur, that we need to increase our eye protection in the Machine 14 area.

                I was just going to have Bob order safety glasses for everyone unless someone else has a better idea.

Rick: How about if we just put out a box of glasses for people that have to work in that area?

Manager: That sounds good, Rick. Could you get the other leads together and make sure that everyone on the shifts complies?

Bob: How about if we paint a line on the floor to designate where people need to wear the glasses?

Manager: That sounds good. Please go ahead and outline the area, and I'll check it before we paint it permanently in place.

Worker 1: What about those of us who wear glasses already?

Manager: Bob, make sure that what you order fits over people's personal glasses too. Thanks.

I'll get the paperwork together to show that we are complying with the new safety requirements. Anyone else have any questions?

(Pause.)

Thanks, Everyone. Good meeting.

Rick, can I see you in my office about those numbers for today? Thanks.

Bob, let me see what you're ordering and I'll approve it.

(The manager stays to discuss some things with the leads, and people start to shuffle out.)

As you can see from the meeting, there are people whom the manager trusts, but he continues to validate that the trust is warranted. Again, these are the *most prevalent* behaviors of 2nd epiphany managers. Let's take a closer look at the 2nd epiphany manager's organization to see how these behaviors play out.

Behaviors in 2nd Epiphany-Managed Organizations

In this organization, most people just do their jobs and get on with life when they aren't at the job site. It's not an organization that you get emotionally invested in; in fact, if you do, you will be disappointed. Well, you'll be disappointed if you are not one of the chosen few, anyway. If you talk to people in a 2nd-epiphany organization, you will get different answers to the question "How do you feel things are going?" From the people who have gained the trust of the manager, the organization is doing well; from the people who have not distinguished themselves, the answer you get will be quite different. In my experience, the ratio is about one trusted person to every ten or so. Be careful. If the manager supplies the people to whom you speak, your evaluation of the organization could be skewed.

Here, generally, are the types of reflective behaviors that are seen in 2nd-epiphany-managed organizations:

It's Just another Day

If the 2nd epiphany manager's principal goal is to maintain things in control, then the array of behaviors we've seen is their principal means of accomplishing it. Trusting a very limited number of people to take independent action is one way the 2nd epiphany manager controls the pace of change in the organization – and the other people who have not earned trust are merely workers that need to be monitored. But, generally speaking, people don't work well in these environments. They will comply; but as far as being engaged, contributing members of the organization, they will not invest themselves in that way.

And why should they be engaged? Working in a regulated and stable environment isn't exactly inspiring. When the pace of change is barely recognizable, one day blends into the next. People who have been bold enough to suggest ideas often experience everything from mild neglect to outright dismissal of their ideas as unworkable, unacceptable, or not good enough. Even if they submit a great idea, if it requires too much change, it will be entirely disregarded. Most people conclude that it is pointless to try because they see that the 2nd epiphany manager won't listen to them anyway. Naturally, when they feel ignored and marginalized, it marks the end of any effort to provide more ideas. And so it goes in the 2nd epiphany organization: Ideas and suggestions go up, but nothing comes back – *it's just another day.*

Just Trying To Do My Job

With a 2nd epiphany manager, people are siloed and just concentrate on doing their jobs. They may feel some flexibility about how they do their work, but since there is no incentive to innovate, they spend their time looking out for Number 1. They may have also learned that they can actually get in trouble by venturing outside their assigned area without prior approval. And while it is rare, a 2nd epiphany manager may even decide to make an example of anyone that operates beyond their silo because meddling could disrupt workflow and even result in awareness that could spark change. The message comes through loud and clear: Do just what you are told within your assigned area.

Normally, the organization is not this oppressive. The more common situation is a kind of mild neglect. But as you can imagine, this type of behavior can have a very detrimental effect on an organization.

Lack of Ownership

Ask someone who is responsible for the process or task and the typical response points to someone else: "The Safety Department is responsible for that," or Maintenance, or Operations. While they understand that they have a part in the process or task, that's as far as it goes. The 2nd epiphany manager usually keeps authority close to the vest. And whether it is by design or simply because the manager doesn't communicate very well, the people in the organization are often in the dark when it comes to understanding the larger issues. So the result is that the 2nd epiphany manager retains authority and, consequently, the people in his charge have zero ownership of the process. After all, why would you agree to be responsible for something if you have no authority to influence it? But this is very frustrating to anyone whose natural work ethic is to take pride and ownership in their work product, not to mention how inefficient and ineffective an organization can be when people don't take ownership of their work.

This is fundamental to the organization's behavior. Where there is no authority, there is also no ownership. If authority is given to others by this manager, it is usually accompanied with careful monitoring. So even if you have the authority, if you make a decision that runs counter to what the manager would do, you will find yourself in an uncomfortable position with this manager. People in this organization are often on the defensive when things go wrong, and you can hear it in their responses: "I just followed the procedure" or "That's the way we were told to do it." It might not have to be done the manager's way, but it will be done somebody's way, and you can expect that *the way* has been approved by this manager.

The Place Where Dead Wood Grows

When you compare this organization to the 1st epiphany manager's organization, this one offers a much more tolerable existence. Very little is given and very little is expected of anyone in the organization, so a lot of people go there to retire in place. For them, work is just a means to an end and there is a certain tranquility in knowing that, if you do your job to the minimum requirements, you will be just fine.

The real problem with this situation is that the resistance to change forces talent out of the organization almost by means of natural selection. With so little room to create and innovate, anyone that hopes to be more than a simple cog in the organization's operation will become restless and leave to find an outlet for their talents. I don't mean to imply that people who do well in the 2nd epiphany manager's organization are not talented, do not enjoy challenges or desire change; they just don't do it at work. The people who are left in the organization are those who work for a living as opposed to those who live for work. And with so much of its human capital drained or left unused, change is something that is done *to* the organization and never brought about *by* the organization.

Factions and Towers

The 2nd-epiphany-managed organization is perceived as being a faction unto itself, existing in a tower that has a mote and drawbridge, and is somewhat labyrinthine once inside. In a very real sense, the 2nd epiphany manager erects the walls of a fiefdom, controlling what goes in and out of the organization – and the workers adopt and promote this organizational persona. It works for them. Everything goes through the gatekeeper, and consequently there is not a lot of interaction or communication between employees or other factions. Instead, there are proscribed processes to handle communication and tasks. The workers spend a lot of time maintaining and controlling resources (as opposed to being innovative) and refer all requests to the manager because virtually no one else has authority to make decisions.

Second epiphany managers can be found at all levels, from first-line supervisor to vice president. It is not uncommon to have several 2nd epiphany managers in a company, and that would be when the company starts to resemble large silos. It's the kind of company that needs five signatures to requisition a desk for a new employee or would institute a policy of using TPS reports as in the movie "*Office Space*." It's all easily justified by saying something to the effect of "I need to control my resources to accomplish the tasks that are important."

Not My Job

In a 2nd-epiphany-managed organization, everyone from the boss on down knows their place and what they should do. If you ask someone to do something outside of that, the likely answer would be "That's not my job." The request is simply deflected to someone else because there is no ownership in this group. It would not be uncommon to find people in 2nd-epiphany-managed organizations to be doing the same job for a decade or more. Not that there is anything wrong with that, but I would question whether this person was offered the chance to grow.

While the division of labor as shown by Adam Smith in "*An Inquiry into the Nature and Causes of the Wealth of Nations*" allows us to produce more than we could ever hope to produce independently, there is a point at which that increase in productivity stops and even reverts backwards. When the people who do certain tasks are in limited supply or at maximum capacity, the total output of the organization will be limited. As an example, when you have ten carpenters but only one iron worker making nails, your organization will only be able to produce what the one iron worker can provide.

In a 2nd-epiphany-managed organization, the capacity of the group is limited by its most limited resource, the people with the official critical skills. In many instances, this will be the manager with approval authority. In some cases, it will be specific trades or people with specific training and certifications. Whatever the case, in this organization, some limiting factor will be used as a common excuse.

Everyone Is Rated Above Average

One of the most interesting phenomena of 2nd-epiphany-managed organizations is that almost all of the performance ratings are above average. Why is that?

Remembering that 2nd epiphany managers like to be in control, it follows that they must also eliminate as much conflict as possible. It is basic human nature to believe that each of us is special in some way. But while we certainly are unique, the truth is that half of us are below average in any task, with half of us being above the norm. Simple statistics bear this out, but we really don't appreciate being labeled "below average" or "average" even if that is the truth. People react negatively to the idea that their performance is less than perfect, and being referred to as "average" or "below average" is particularly difficult to hear. So when it comes to performance-rating time, 2nd epiphany managers often find it easier to rate everyone that meets the minimum requirements as "above average" at the least.

This can be justified by saying that everyone in their group does better than expected – but how could that really be true? It's how they measure output. Usually in the organization expectations of performance are published. The group normally exceeds these expectations, so they must be performing above the expected norm; hence, they are rated above average.

———————————————————

Overall, the 2nd-epiphany-managed organization may not be a bad place to work. Issues are usually handled fairly, but in general, it is not a very exciting place to be. The theme is control and consistency: No rapid changes, no surprises. People who have entrepreneurial or creative spirits will not be happy and will most likely leave. People who have a drive to grow, thirst for learning, and like change will also be looking to leave eventually.

If you spend time in a 2nd-epiphany-managed organization, expect to hear things like "That's the way it's always been done," "Don't rock the boat," or "Joe did it that way. So if it's good enough for him, it's good enough for us." But don't expect to be part of anything unique or groundbreaking because, again, change happens *to* this organization; it's not driven from within.

Working For a 2nd Epiphany Manager

You either like working for a 2nd epiphany manager or you don't. While almost no one likes to work for the 1st epiphany manager, the 2nd epiphany manager is tolerable and, in some cases, makes a comfortable environment for some. But with this manager, you must work to earn their trust; and it is important to recognize that it will take concerted effort, sometimes on many different fronts, to create the kind of favorable impression that will lead your 2nd epiphany manager to put more trust in you. However, unlike the 1st epiphany manager, this one will actually give you some authority and responsibility if they think you are ready for it. Regardless of your situation, though, there are some things you can do to gain favorable attention, garner respect, and improve your manager's overall perception of your trustworthiness.

In addition, these actions will help the 2nd epiphany manager on their journey to becoming a 3rd epiphany manager – *if* the manager is ready or open to that situation. The major difference between a 2nd epiphany manager and a 3rd epiphany manager is an open mind. If you try some of these actions and receive pushback or are questioned as to why you are asking, then you are most likely dealing with a manager who is not ready to take the next step in the journey.

Ask About the Direction and Goals of the Group

Asking a 2nd epiphany manager about the direction or goals of the organization does a couple things: First, it helps you determine where they are in their journey. If they answer with a question that is designed to deflect rather than clarify, such as, "Why do you want to know?" or "Your lead will answer that question," you can be fairly confident that they are not ready to move beyond where they are. If they provide you with number-based goals only, it's an indication that they are probably ensconced in their 2nd epiphany level as well.

It is generally a good sign if they pause and think before they answer – and it may be that you have given them an opportunity to start to think differently, which is certainly a great outcome. They may simply regurgitate what they have heard other management say word for word or they may attempt to paraphrase the company's vision statement for you, and these responses likely signal that the manager is not ready to move beyond the 2nd epiphany. But it could also mean that they were caught off-guard and need more time to process that line of thinking.

Regardless of the answer you get, however, be ready to follow up with a question of how you can help reach the goals. This will identify you as a person that cares and is willing to help. Of course, you need to be prepared to follow through once you have their attention, and that means performing to the standard and level of expectation of the manager, not your own standard. Sometimes that may be very different than what you think it is, so it is necessary to be clear what the expectations are.

Ask For Feedback

Asking for feedback is another way to "get on their radar," so to speak – and the answer will educate you about what your manager is interested in and looks at, as well as their thoughts and concerns about your work in particular. You may have to ask specific questions about the things you do – "Are my reports meeting your needs? What can I do to make them better for you?" – but this can help you determine if the area you asked about is a concern for them and, if it is, you can find out how to help them, something that they will notice and appreciate if you follow through.

And since this manager dislikes conflict, if you ask for feedback and the answer contains anything that is not appreciation for a superior job, then you know you have room for improvement and should be taking action in any area that is identified. But more importantly, asking for feedback usually sets up an opportunity for more productive dialogue in the future. If you implement the feedback you're given and the manager sees improvement as a result, they are more likely to try to provide feedback again.

Volunteer To Own the Problem/System/Process

With the 2nd epiphany manager, it is all about earning trust. So if you have the opportunity to volunteer to be responsible for a specific problem, process, or system, you should do that. It will show the manager that you can take the initiative and that you can be trusted with it. And again, be clear about what the expectations are so you can meet them.

When you take ownership of an issue or situation, you must provide timely feedback for the status. This manager's personal mantra is "trust but verify." And if you can help them by providing the information so they can verify things, you will go a long way to earn their trust. You will also earn the ability to suggest new ideas about how things should be operated or responded to. You may gain authority over the issue or situation in addition, but with this manager you must have patience.

Ask To Teach a Class on Something for the Organization

In the spirit of gaining the manager's trust, ask to teach a class on something for the organization. By doing this, you identify yourself as an expert in the subject matter. This provides an opportunity for the 2nd epiphany manager to see that the people they manage have in-depth knowledge and skills.

It gives you the opportunity to gain credibility with the people in your group, awakens your manager to the brain trust resource, and can help you gain the manager's trust. From my perspective, it's a win-win situation – if you can make it relevant, useful, and timely.

Go Back To School and Share with the Group

In our careers, there are times when we attend classes, workshops, or seminars where the latest and greatest information is shared. Use these opportunities to take information back to the group. Ask to share with the group, and hopefully you will reap the benefits that were outlined above when you teach the class.

This has the added benefit of providing different industry perspectives to the 2nd epiphany manager's reality. If they are willing to open their mind to the opportunity to learn, they will see that others are working on the same problems that the group is struggling with. It can also provide insight to how others have solved these problems.

Go Beyond the Call of Duty

Under the 2nd epiphany manager, it is especially important to go beyond the call of duty. If you want to have a chance to impress this manager, you need to do something that will get their attention. Things like documenting the solution to a problem, designing an improved process, and volunteering can all work toward this goal of recognition.

Quick Caveat: Don't do something that the manager may not be comfortable with your doing. If you do something unpredictable or out of the ordinary, they may react unfavorably. So when you decide to go above and beyond, get their permission first or at least understand their limits.

Speak At a Conference

Taking the opportunity to speak to a group of peers and to be recognized as an expert in your chosen field will go a long way to help this manager invest their trust in you. The goal is to have the 2nd epiphany manager see you as someone that they can rely on when they have need for advice in a certain area of the business; but as you can see, it takes time and considerable effort to build this type of reputation. Speaking at a conference is a powerful way to gain this sort of recognition, but your patience and commitment to earn their trust over time speaks volumes. Soon the 2nd epiphany manager will consider your opinion in other areas as well. For your effort, you will have gained trust and appreciation and the manager will have gained someone that they can go to for answers.

Write a White Paper

Writing a white paper for your company or other respected periodical has the same effect as speaking at a conference or seminar of your peers. The article will show your manager that you have a certain level of expertise in an area of the business or operation that is valuable. Again, remember that how much the manager appreciates the body of work will depend on their opinion and perception of it. If it has been peer-judged and accepted for publication in a respected journal, then your manager will probably have more respect for your work.

While having a juried, peer-reviewed article in a respected journal is nice, it isn't the only way to win this manager's respect. You could just as easily write a lesson plan that is accepted by the training department. Creating a simple instructional paper in the company's website, blog, or publication can also help open your manager's eyes to the value you are providing to the company. Learn what is important to your manager and consider how you can support them to gain acceptance and trust in their eyes.

Thank Your Manager for Doing Something That Helps You

If the manager does something that makes it easier to do your job or makes your life easier in some way, thank them. Thanks can take the form of a simple note, comment, or email and is usually best if personal rather than public. While thanking the manager in front of the entire group can be good, it can also be seen from a different perspective (which is not always beneficial). The best kind of appreciation is something that is immediate to the situation, specific, and sincere. It doesn't have to be given in the context of some large event.

Thanking the 2nd epiphany manager lets them know that you are paying attention and that they are making a difference. It focuses the manager's attention on the fact that their actions affect other people's lives and performance – and this is a key realization if the manager is to become a leader.

Treat Your Manager as an Equal with a Different Job

While it may not be true of all 2nd epiphany managers, I have found it to be the case for enough of them to recommend the following action: Treat your manager as an equal. Managers and leaders are really no different from anyone else, other than that they have different responsibilities and authority. Their job may be different than yours, but it isn't any more or less important than yours. And while managers can affect the business, there are many non-managers who can also affect the business. A company attorney, QA inspector, product assembly person, salesperson, even a receptionist can affect a company for better or worse.

Still, you shouldn't take this as license to be disrespectful. All people deserve respect. But in your dealings with the 2nd epiphany manager, keep the perspective that they have a job to do and you have yours. Both of your behaviors affect each other's performance and in this perspective you are both equals.

Human interaction is complex and rarely straightforward, so these actions are offered as examples and suggestions that need to be tailored to fit your specific situation. It takes a fair amount of sensitivity and thought to understand the best course of action when working to help someone see a different path or change their perspective. But in general, be patient and helpful. When you hear your manager discussing a problem or see that they are staying late to work on a project, ask to see if you can help. If something needs to be monitored by your manager and you have experience and knowledge in that area, offer to help out in the monitoring. All these things show that you care and will place you both in the same position of working on a common problem.

As I mentioned before, the majority of managers I meet are at this stage. A person can become very comfortable in this 2nd epiphany world, either as a manager or as part of the group being managed. But comfortable as it may be, the 2nd epiphany manager typically hasn't learned to tap into the human capital of their group to make it more effective and efficient. By implementing some of the suggestions outlined above, a person can open up opportunities for the manager to see the potential of this largely unused human resource. It takes courage to effect change, especially when control and stability are so highly valued by the manager at this level; but if the manager is able to experience the 3rd epiphany, the organization will grow with them.

Pathways to the 3rd Epiphany

I'm willing to bet that no one is going to come up to you and tell you that you are a 2nd epiphany manager. And it should be that way. The path of learning to be a great leader is one of self discovery, for the most part. It is defined by moments of enlightenment and epiphanies. As you look at the section on 2nd epiphany manager behaviors and, more importantly, the section on organizational reflective behaviors, make an honest assessment. Does your group's behavior resemble any of the behaviors I've mentioned? If it does, then there are still vestiges of 2nd-epiphany-management behavior.

In each of the pathway sections, I outline behaviors that can be helpful to any level of management. The following actions are designed to help you discover truths about how people react to different leadership behaviors. I hope that by following the suggestions you will open your mind to new possibilities and see how you and your group can grow and perform. They are designed to help you find the untapped resources in your group by giving your people the chance to meet new challenges.

Be aware that if your organization has been operating under a certain set of conditions for many years or even months, there will be resistance to change. You may have to try these behaviors many times to allow people the chance to get used to the new culture that you are trying to implement. Yes, I did say "culture." You as the manager and leader of your group set the culture by your behavior. So let's continue on the task of making situations that can bring insight to you as you explore new possibilities.

Stop Asking How and Start Asking What

I was a facilities manager at a high-tech manufacturing plant. One of our chemical delivery systems was starting to leak and needed to be replaced. It used a very hazardous chemical that could cause burns and permanent damage if someone were to come in contact with it. This chemical was a key component in our plant's processes; without it, there would be no production.

My initial thoughts were to bring in experienced contractors to do the work. I even contacted several to get bids. But I didn't think to ask my group "What should we do?" Luckily for me, one of my trusted leads stepped up and stated that we could do the work with our current workforce. I was asking "*How* should we do this?" instead of the larger question of "*What* should we do?" I was actually startled by the boldness of the plan; but after I did some investigation and additional planning, I believed in the plan.

The fact is that we avoided any downtime (whereas the shortest downtime offered by a contractor was 3 days), and we saved over $300,000 from the lowest bid. The system was replaced in place with no incidents or downtime, all because one person in my group wasn't afraid to answer the larger question of "what" instead of my question of "how."

Ask the larger question, "What should we do?" Let the brain power of the group attack the problem and help you reach a great outcome. When you ask "what," you involve people in the larger picture. They gain insight to the overall goals and expectations of the organization; you gain insight to the group's ability to deliver solutions.

As with anything that requires different behaviors, you will have to work to make this a habit. It may not always produce spectacular results; but we climb mountains one step at a time, and any suggestions that allow us to make progress are good. Be patient with your group. It will take time for them to learn that they can respond, ask for clarification without reprisal, and realize that their opinions are valued.

Be prepared to look at the suggestions with an open mind so that you can find the nuggets within when you ask, "What should we do?" Some suggestions will sound like silliness, but there may be a thread of truth and a path to a real solution in the reply. I have seen groups spend time and effort that exceeded the cost of replacing entire systems because they were stuck in repair mode instead of looking at the bigger picture. When the group was asked about the repair of the equipment, one person asked, "What does is cost for a new one?" That brought inquiry that showed that it was indeed less costly to replace the unit instead of repairing them. If you are careful to ask "what" instead of "how," you just might find that your group has great ideas and suggestions.

Assign Owners of Processes/Systems/Areas

Assign people in the group to become owners of the processes, systems, or areas. With this, you have to give them the authority to make changes, control, and maintain what you have assigned them. Remember that responsibility must be balanced with an appropriate level of authority to accomplish what you gave them to do. This is not an excuse to deflect your responsibilities, but rather to engage people in the goals and mission of the group.

When you assign ownership of the area to a person, make sure that you also give them the performance expectations along with the authority and responsibility. Change your behavior to reflect that they own what you gave them. Go to them for information about it; treat them as the point of contact for anything that has to do with their charges. Refer those that deal with the assigned responsibility to talk to the person that you put in charge of it. Only get involved if performance is not meeting expectations, they are not responsive to inquiries, or their charges are performing better than expected (give credit where credit is due).

When you properly give ownership of something to a person, you give them trust – trust in their abilities, trust in the outcome, and trust that they will make good decisions. You engage their intelligence, experience, and motivate them by the trust (which is a form of appreciation). What you get in return is the engagement of the whole person, or at least enough of them to get the job done in a way that meets your expectations.

Giving ownership of processes, systems, and areas is one of the most powerful ways that I know to engage people into the mission of the group. It is a technique that can bring great rewards, but you have to be willing to support and let your people grow in these responsibilities. You cannot just "fire and forget." Your people will need help and guidance when you do this. So be prepared to engage with them, learn something from them, and be inspired by them. Properly done, this can be very much a win-win proposition.

Articulate a Clear Vision and Mission for the Group

One of the requirements of engaging anyone's intellect is to provide them with a vision of some future state. Where are you trying to go? What are you trying to accomplish? Envisioning a future state allows people to reflect upon their skills, knowledge, and experience to determine how they can interact to help it occur if they view the future state as desirable. Simply said, if they like what you're trying to accomplish, they will engage their whole person to help you – so long as you let them.

To do this, you must articulate a future state – a vision of what you are trying to accomplish or build. This can be a vision statement or some kind of document that outlines the desired future state. This vision can be transitory or permanent in nature. If your vision is to be the best baseball team, then this guides everyone on what they have to do and everyone works toward that end. If your vision is to have an accident-free mining operation, then people will put their resources to that goal.

While a vision statement is about a future state, the mission statement is what you are about today. Your vision can be integrated into your mission statement or other statement of intent; but regardless of the method, it has to be visible, easy to understand, and mean something personally to each individual in your group. This is something that you don't have to develop with anyone else, but it's beneficial if you do. The people in your group – and any managers, in particular – should know what your intentions are. They will either agree with it or not. But the selection of a vision/mission should be the job of the leader.

Notice that I used the word "leader" as opposed to "manager." The development and articulation of a vision and mission is the first thing that leaders do. Managers, hold people to requirements and certain behaviors, but leaders inspire people to action with a great vision and mission. I suspect that it will take you some practice to get a vision and mission that is both inspirational and personally meaningful to your people. This is where your mentor and peers can help you.

In my opinion, these are some examples of good vision and mission statements:

Archer Daniels Midland: *To unlock the potential of nature to improve the quality of life.*

Bristol-Myers Squibb Company: *To discover, develop and deliver innovative medicines that help patients prevail over serious diseases.*

Ford Motor Company: *We are a global family with a proud heritage passionately committed to providing personal mobility for people around the world.*

Microsoft: *We work to help people and businesses throughout the world realize their full potential.*

Nike, Inc.: *To bring inspiration and innovation to every athlete in the world.*

Google: *To organize the world's information and make it universally accessible and useful.*

And of course one of what not to do …

"The Company's primary objective is to maximize long-term stockholder value, while adhering to the laws of the jurisdictions in which it operates and at all times observing the highest ethical standards."

Can you tell what this company does? Neither could I. It was a food company, by the way. It looks to me to be written by a lawyer for lawyers.

While these are company examples, you can write mission and vision statements for any size organization, including yourself. I actually know people who have personal mission and vision statements.

The basic information that needs to be conveyed is: What does the future look like and what part do we play in that future? There are many books on this subject, and I recommend that you find one that resonates with what you want to accomplish in your organization. Remember that doing this is one of the first steps that any leader takes to inspire people.

Get To Know Each of the People Who Work For You

While you don't have to invite everyone over for a backyard barbeque, take the time to learn about your people. What skills, knowledge, and experience do they have? What other jobs have they held? What helps them be successful, and where do they want to go in their careers? What inspires them?

When you learn about people, you learn their abilities, and the breadth and depth of their knowledge. What resources do they bring with them and how might they be able to help the group? Were they instructors or teachers in the past? Do they have in-depth knowledge of the processes your organization uses? It helps you know what assets are available to you within your own group. And you might be surprised at what you learn.

I was surprised to learn that one of my people was a qualified locksmith. His skill became a very valuable asset that helped us reduce costs and our dependence on area contractors.

Taking time to learn about the people in your group works both ways. When we were involved in a structural upgrade project, my group was surprised that their manager was a qualified welder. As a result, they didn't need to rely upon a local weld shop to get the more critical welding done. This helped reduce the cost of the project and earned recognition and awards for the group.

Spend time with your people, get to know them, and learn what assets you really have. You may be surprised at the resources you actually have available to you.

Develop a Catalog of Skills and Knowledge

As you get to know your people, document their work-related skills and knowledge. A catalog of skills and knowledge can become very important when you are tasked with abnormal challenges or situations. It could serve as a great guide to know to whom you can turn when the situation arises. You can also use it to identify those with great skills that can train others or to identify weaknesses within the entire group. It's very helpful as a guide when hiring to identify candidates whose skills complement those that already exist in your group.

One thing you shouldn't use the catalog for is to identify weaknesses in people for training or performance enhancement. Unless it directly affects the work performance that a person was hired for, your use of this tool in that manner can have serious adverse effects. As an example, discovering that your engineer has some serious weaknesses in marketing and sales and then trying to send them to training will probably not work. People are generally predisposed toward certain professions or industries based upon their life experiences and preferences. Forcing them to learn something that they do not have a natural tendency toward is like teaching a left-handed person to be right-handed. So only use the tool at a group or organizational level.

Give Feedback to Each Person At Least Weekly

This action isn't a call to do some formal write-up or go through a checklist with anyone. It's a call to make it personal with each member of your group. When you lead an organization or group, you more often than not lead one person at a time. Personal interaction with each member of your team will help you get to know what each is doing, the issues with which they struggle, what is making their life easier, and how they think and react to various situations. You can learn a lot about them and their abilities in the process.

In addition, providing feedback can help you assess how what they are doing affects the organization's ability to reach its goals, and what you might be able to do to help. It forces you to learn about them and their situation and gives you the opportunity to show that you care as you react to their situation. Leadership is about developing relationships, and this is an avenue to promote just that.

Feedback can take the form of a simple attagirl or attaboy but must address a specific action or behavior that you observed or have direct knowledge about. Show them that you are paying attention and that you care about them professionally.

You can also use this as an opportunity to get feedback on your behavior and support. What can you do better? What can you do to help out? You might be surprised what they see and how they perceive your actions. If they take the opportunity to give you feedback, remember to accept it for what it is – a perception of what they have heard or observed – and thank them for it. Remember that it takes courage to give feedback to a manager. And realize that no perception is wrong; it is usually only the interpretation or misunderstanding of actions without knowing the situation as you do. Regardless, if someone brings up feedback for you, take it under investigation at least. Again, show people that you are paying attention, care about them professionally, and value their perceptions.

Find Reasons to Appreciate Each Person

> *"Appreciation is a wonderful thing. It makes what is excellent in others belong to us as well."*
>
> *Voltaire*

One of the universal motivators is appreciation. Find a reason to appreciate everyone every day. Catch excellence when it happens. Be prepared to find people doing great things and make sure that you make them aware that you noticed and appreciate what they have done.

It doesn't take a formal event or even some type of plaque just to say thank you. The rules of appreciation are:

- *Make it immediate*

Make sure that the appreciation is timely so that the person can easily connect the desired behavior with the appreciation received. This also helps others see the relationship between behavior and appreciation.

- *Make it appropriate*

Appreciation needs to reflect the perceived effort. As an example, take the sale of $1 million of services. If the person is a vice president, it might be appropriate to just say thank you (assuming that they are responsible for hundreds of millions in sales). On the other hand, if the person is a front line salesperson and the million-dollar sale doubles the company's revenues for the year, a trip to Hawaii might be more appropriate. The key to this is perceived effort. This is in the eyes of the person doing the work.

- *Make it sincere*

Insincere appreciation can do damage to an organization. It is perceived as outright lying. If you are going to give appreciation, it needs to be seen as a reward for something that brought value to the group.

If you follow these rules and work to catch people going above and beyond, this too will become a valued organizational behavior and will integrate into the culture.

I can't over-emphasize the importance of appreciation. It is one of the few universal human constants. It transcends all cultures and age groups, meaning that there is no human that doesn't need to be appreciated. The trick is to find out what they want to be appreciated for and how they expect to be appreciated, and getting to know each of the people who work for you will help you determine that.

The next epiphany and the realizations that come with it will open your mind to the tremendous potential of people. It takes a leap of faith, some understanding of why people behave the way they do (especially ourselves), and how groups behave – which can be very different from the way individuals would choose to behave). You have certainly made great progress, having come this far, and you are taking the first steps to become a leader instead of a manager.

"I consider my ability to arouse enthusiasm among men the greatest asset I possess. The way to develop the best that is in a man is by appreciation and encouragement."

Charles Schwab

The 2nd Epiphany

"If you go through life convinced that your way is always best, all the new ideas in the world will pass you by."

Akio Morita
Co-founder of Sony

Chapter 4

The 3rd Epiphany

"Synergy" is a term I hear a lot when people talk about organizations and how they behave. You may have heard this term being bandied about by organizational performance experts and consultants. The Wikipedia defines "synergy" as "… two or more things functioning together to produce a result not independently obtainable" (Wikipedia.org, 2012). I like this definition, because it actually describes quite well what can happen when we get people engaged at a high level within a group.

With synergy, you get things like the iPhone®, the transistor, men walking on the moon, the Declaration of Independence, Starbucks, cars that get 50-plus miles to the gallon, the Internet, polio vaccines, artificial hearts, and disease-resistant wheat. When people get together to solve problems or meet a need, sometimes really great things come out of it. But this only occurs when the organizational environment is right. This is what most leaders try to do and great leaders accomplish, but it starts with a simple realization …

The 3rd Epiphany

These people are actually smarter than I am.

When this philosophy is adopted across an organization, the fundamental shift in tenets transforms the organization from reactive to proactive – which is exactly what creates the environment that supports synergy within groups. Many organizational improvement programs were built upon the philosophy that everyone has something valuable to contribute – Total Quality Management and Quality Circles, popular in the 1980s, to name two – and the great organizations still base their policies and processes around the basic idea.

But for the manager, this simple realization is the fundamental shift that marks the transition from manager to leader. The manager that has experienced this epiphany begins to value diversity in that they realize that every person represents a great resource of skill, knowledge, and experience. When they look at the group of people they lead, they see huge potential and will want to explore what everyone knows and how to get everyone involved. They have seen what happens when you engage the whole person and tap into passions, and this experience changes everything about how they view, manage, and lead organizations.

Having witnessed the great power of the crowd to accomplish things, the 3rd epiphany manager seeks to engage everyone. When the 3rd epiphany takes hold, they drop control as the primary driver in their behavior because they recognize that people want to get involved and do the right thing. So they work to make it easy for their people to participate. They equate participation with increased organizational effectiveness and they see people for the resource that they are and appreciate them.

This newfound belief can work to their detriment in different ways, however, when taken too far. One example is, when people don't meet the 3rd epiphany manager's expectations around participation, they may be mistakenly viewed as non-team players or people who don't fit in. They may even isolate those who, by their behavior, don't seem to want to contribute within the group. After all, who wouldn't want to participate?

As managers grow into leaders, their behaviors become more a composite of all the behaviors that we have seen so far, and it would be a mistake to think that any one behavior is a dominant predictor of where a person is. It is more telling to notice how a manager behaves under high stress and very low stress. In high-stress situations, you get a feel for where the manager is most comfortable, believes they can create the most value, and has the most experience. In low-stress situations, you will see the manager venture out into new experiences. First and 2nd epiphany managers sometimes try things that resemble 3rd and 4th epiphany behaviors, but that may be under the direction of a superior. The aggregate of general tendencies is a more useful gauge to assess where we are on the path to leadership.

Behavioral Traits of the 3rd Epiphany Manager

> *"What we need to do is learn to work in the system, by which I mean that everybody, every team, every platform, every division, every component is there not for individual competitive profit or recognition, but for contribution to the system as a whole on a win-win basis."*

> *W. Edward Deming*

Third epiphany managers focus primarily on diversity and group interaction in an attempt to reach continuous synergy in their processes – which is impossible to do, by the way. This manager constantly poses questions to groups, both formally and informally. They build processes that make group interaction the norm and even a requirement because they are so determined to engage everyone to obtain the greatest benefit from their collective brainpower.

Let's Get A Meeting Together To Discuss ...

Driven by the firm belief that everyone together is smarter than any one individual, the 3rd epiphany manager will naturally want to get the group together to discuss situations. After all, meetings are the standard way of doing business. If you try to get in to discuss something with this manager, more often than not they will listen and then recommend that it be brought up at the next meeting.

Sharing

One of the reasons to have so many meetings is to share information. Third epiphany managers like to keep everyone informed and in the loop, expecting that their combined intellect will provide the solution to any obstacle they face. If everyone knows what is happening, someone may come up with a better way to improve efficiency and effectiveness. These managers share group performance data, financial data, and outside data with everyone. Want to know something? Just ask.

Idea-Of-The-Month Club

Unlike the 2nd epiphany manager, who sees ideas as disruptive, the 3rd epiphany manager loves new ideas and actively solicits them from the group. They encourage people to bring their brains to work and participate, and will find ways to appreciate the effort. There might even be awards for the best and most ideas. All in all, because this manager really does appreciate ideas and the people who present them, it can be nice to work for a 3rd epiphany manager.

But this mindset can lead to an idea-of-the-month culture where the organization is actually in perpetual-development mode. New ideas are constantly being sponsored and promulgated to the group in meetings. The 3rd epiphany manager is forever assigning groups and committees to work on feasibility, improvements, or implementation. Sometimes the ideas come in so quickly that the group's resources don't allow for proper evaluation or implementation.

Committees – Lots of Committees

Naturally, then, one of the main activities for the 3rd epiphany manager is to commission committees to investigate, solve, or monitor. They will request that you join a committee. ("Request" is a euphemism in this case.) They just like the idea that everyone participates or at least has the opportunity to participate.

When there is an idea to explore or a problem to be solved, convening a committee is their customary plan of attack. There will be committees for everything. This manager will create a committee for the Christmas party, the organization's mission statement, where people should park, when breaks should be taken, and even what color to paint the building.

One interesting note: If the manager convenes a committee of consultants, it is actually 2nd epiphany behavior, not 3rd epiphany behavior. But suffice it to say that, if a group has more than three committees, its manager is fully committed to the 3rd epiphany.

Questionnaires and Polls

What is your opinion? That's what this manager wants to know. Questionnaires are distributed and polls are taken, either directly or indirectly through companies that specialize in these services. (SurveyMonkey.com comes to mind.) They report the poll's results in the committee meetings they call, and there will be discussion to validate the results and see what people think.

This manager commonly believes that the majority opinion is the right way to go, but problems occur when they start to depend on committees to make decisions that they could – and should – be making themselves.

Decisions by Vote or Consensus

All these brains can't be wrong. Having created the environment where good decisions can be made, the 3rd epiphany manager will initiate discussion, solicit opinion, and call upon the group to vote for the best course of action.

But belief in the wisdom of the crowd sets up some interesting dynamics for organizations. The fact is that committees are naturally risk-averse, and if anything is to be accomplished in committee, groupthink usually ensures it will be done little bits at a time. As John Kenneth Galbraith said, "Meetings are a great trap. Soon you find yourself trying to get agreement and then the people who disagree come to think they have a right to be persuaded. However, they are indispensable when you don't want to do anything."

Other interesting scenarios can develop when decisions by vote or consensus reigns. Of course, it's easy when everyone agrees and there is consensus. But what happens if everyone agrees but the manager? It's an intriguing possibility, and the answer may surprise you. It is actually not uncommon to see the

3rd epiphany manager defer to the group's decision because they value their opinion so highly. And perhaps even more unexpectedly when this is the case, the manager may find that they have a difficult time selling the idea if, to begin with, they were never truly convinced of its merit.

So what if the vote is 50/50 or something very close? The 3rd epiphany manager will most likely send it back to committee for further study and fact-finding to reach a more persuasive argument one way or the other. They may even convene a new committee.

Paralysis by Analysis

As shown above, when a vote or poll shows no clear-cut decision path, the 3rd epiphany manager often refers things to a committee or group to find more facts or conduct more research. This is where analysis paralysis can set in. This special form of active inactivity describes the continuous evaluation and study of a situation that never leads to an outcome, just further investigation.

Third epiphany managers cause their organizations to suffer this malady because they depend on the thoughts and opinions of the group and either want or need consensus to move forward – or to move in any direction for that matter. While analysis paralysis can happen to managers at any epiphany, it is most commonly seen in 3rd epiphany managers and rarely seen among 1st epiphany managers. Fourth epiphany leaders usually recognize the situation and immediately correct it or prevent it from occurring in the first place.

Trusting the Masses and Clouded Vision

The 3rd epiphany manager can become very comfortable trusting that everyone in the group wants to do the right thing.

And, for the most part, it works out well for all concerned. Most employees do know their jobs and work perfectly well without management, but it can also lead to apathy on the job. The trust and independence this manager gives their people can be viewed in different ways. The manager sees that people are doing just fine on their own, but the employees may interpret it as receiving little interaction from the manager.

Trust in the wisdom of the masses can produce some interesting consequences in the 3rd epiphany manager's organization as well. For example, the individuals in the 3rd-epiphany-managed organization usually have a difficult time articulating the vision and mission of the group. What you find, is the vision is different from person to person, and everyone seems to have a different idea about where the group is going when asked. This is because the 3rd epiphany manager lists feelings or emotional states for goals. Their mission statements include words like "honesty," "innovative," and "world's best." But these words are inherently vague because each person ascribes their own meaning to them. Exactly how do you measure these goals?

Respect for All

One of the great attributes of the 3rd epiphany manager is their respect for all. This is a product of the epiphany itself, the firm belief that everyone is valuable and has something worthwhile to contribute. This manager takes time to listen to everyone and ensures that they have opportunity to participate in almost everything.

They also champion the causes of diversity and the integration of different cultures, values, and views. Their organizations reflect the societies they live in, and they will stand up and fight for equal opportunity. The 3rd epiphany manager may be the first to put people into non-traditional roles.

The Open Management Style

For the most part, the 3rd epiphany manager believes in and practices an open management style. They believe that transparency is the key to getting the most out of the group and they are not afraid to share their concerns or let you know what they are thinking about. Their group is apprised of situations as they develop, and they freely share their perspectives in meetings where the group will be called upon to help solve the issues.

Their door is actually open, and they invite people to come in and chat about issues and concerns. They may publish these concerns and issues in emails to the group and expect feedback. *They actually want the feedback.* They hope that by showing people what they deal with, that everyone will become involved and help out. As shown before, this manager has a tendency to put things to a vote and hopes to reach consensus. It isn't difficult to find out what this manager is thinking or what's on their minds, if it isn't clear already.

Real Caring

Third epiphany managers really care for the people that work for them. They are concerned about their employees' safety and welfare; they take time to listen to their concerns and honestly try to help or deal with adverse situations. Their interest in their employees' well-being can sometimes even take the form of mentoring. A lot of people enjoy the work environment created by the 3rd epiphany manager.

It is not uncommon for 3rd epiphany managers to support Junior Achievement, Habitat for Humanity, and other charitable organizations. They see it as their duty to encourage their group to participate in these causes as well. They are willing to authorize time off to participate or to engage in activities that support charities.

This genuine concern can sometimes translate into "rules" that make it fair for everyone, even to the point of causing inefficiencies in organizations. I have seen 3rd epiphany managers implement the rule that everyone that applies to a job must be interviewed, even if there are hundreds of applications.

It is easy to see that the focus of this manager is to harness as much of the brain power of the organization as possible. They envision organizations where everyone is engaged, innovating, and being productive. They believe in people and in the wisdom of the crowd. They create organizations that appreciate great ideas, support collaboration, and believe in diversity. As you will see in the next sections, working in a 3rd-epiphany-managed environment has its advantages and is generally very pleasant.

The 3rd Epiphany Manager's Meeting

As in previous chapters, this section provides an example of what a meeting might be like with this kind of manager. There are some profound differences in how this manager conducts the meeting. Examine what they do and how they focus people to come up with a better outcome. Compare this meeting's outcome with the previous managers' meetings. How does this meeting compare to the meetings that you attend?

Same Background & Setting: In an automotive parts manufacturing company employing over a thousand people, a mandatory meeting to discuss new safety requirements is scheduled. Notice of the meeting and a copy of the new safety requirements were sent out by management to the group of eight people a week before the meeting. The new safety requirements are to be implemented no later than four weeks from the meeting date. The meeting is to be held in a meeting room off the factory floor at the start of the shift, 8:00 a.m. The manager is the first-level supervisor.

Manager: (Arriving about 3 minutes late from the last meeting.)

Hi, Everybody. I see that some people aren't here yet. I'll give them a few minutes to join in.

(Glancing over to Bob) Bob, did you see the suggestions that came out of the process improvement committee? I think they've got some great ideas.

(The manager continues to chat with Bob for a few minutes and then notices the time.)

Okay, People. Let's get started.

We have a new memo from the Safety Department that adds some new requirements to what we do. I hope that everyone got a chance to read it. I brought a couple of extra copies if you didn't.

Okay. I'm looking for how we implement this. Who's got ideas?

Rajesh: It looks like Machine Area 14 is the only area affected.

Katie: I agree with Rajesh. I believe that 14 is the only area we need to worry about.

Manager:	Does anyone else have an opinion on which areas this affects?

(Everyone nods or agrees verbally.)

Manager:	Okay, then. It sounds like we are in agreement. So what ideas do we have to address the concern?"
Manny:	Rick and I looked at the area and think that we could just mark it as an area that needs safety glasses so the only time you would need to wear them is when you are in the area.
Katie:	Do people who wear glasses already need to wear safety glasses? Are there some that fit over regular glasses?
Manager:	I don't know. I'm sure that they make them.
Bob:	Isn't the concern that the particles fly off the machine and causes this hazard? Can we build a guard for this?
Manager:	Sounds like we have some great ideas coming up. Bob could chair a committee to investigate the various options and costs associated with them.

Bob, do you think a week is enough time to do that?

Bob:	Yes, I think that we can do that.

(Addressing the group) If you want help out with this, please send me an email stating so. We will get together tomorrow morning at 9:00 a.m. in this same room.

Manager: Thanks, Bob.

               Great. Then we can have them report back to the entire group next week with what they find.

               Good. Then, is there anything else that we need to discuss?

               (The group generally agrees that there is nothing else that they want to bring up now.)

Manager: Good meeting, Everyone. Thank you all.

               (Noticing the time again) Okay. I have my next meeting in 5 minutes and that gives me just enough time to check email. Thanks, People.

               (The manager leaves the meeting room and heads to the next meeting.)

In this example, you can see that the 3rd epiphany manager values the input from each person and wants to make sure that everyone has the opportunity to participate. Things don't move very quickly when you have to include everyone, but this manager reasons that they get better results operating in this fashion. Their guiding philosophy is the good from the many far exceeds the good from the few.

Behaviors in 3rd Epiphany-Managed Organizations

Have you stopped to think how far the ripples of any of these epiphanies can be felt? Taking the 3rd epiphany as an example, this philosophy can even be seen in the architecture of the buildings and the organization's investment in technology. The 3rd-epiphany-managed organization will have many meeting rooms and spaces that promote interaction. Technology and systems will be designed to support collaboration and open communications. Google is the classic example of this. Third-epiphany philosophies are so integrated into the culture at Google that, traditionally, no one has a private office, including the CEO. Every space is designed to promote collaboration, and most decisions are made by consensus. Overall, it is continually rated as one of the best places to work.

As you can see, working at a 3rd–epiphany-managed company has its advantages, but are there any disadvantages? One problem I see sometimes at this level is that implementation of 3rd-epiphany philosophies across large organizations can be difficult. In addition, some 3rd-epiphany-managed organizations tend to lose focus of their mission and goals. But regardless of the size of the organization, the effects of 3rd-epiphany behavior ripple through to encompass almost every aspect of their operation, management philosophy, and practices.

Meetings upon Meetings

Have an idea? Call a meeting. Have a crisis? Call a meeting. Meetings proliferate in the 3rd-epiphany-managed organization, and it is a virtual expectation that everyone will want to contribute and share their experiences and ideas. Consequently, meetings can take upward to 75 percent of your time if you're a manager, only 50 percent of your time if you're a professional, and up to 25 percent of your time regardless of who you are.

Very busy ... Progress?

When you look at a 3rd-epiphany-managed organization, things may seem very busy – but action shouldn't be confused with progress. People may attend a lot of meetings, produce copious reports, and create an endless stream of great ideas; but how do they validate, test, and implement those great ideas? If the organization fails to execute on its plans, does it matter if there is a great program for the submission of ideas or even a great rewards system in place?

The company's mission may be to make widgets, operate power plants, land aircraft, or manufacture new cures for diseases; but the products of the 3rd epiphany organization, in reality, are meetings, reports, and great ideas. Being very busy is one of the ways 3rd-epiphany-managed organizations lose focus of their mission and goals.

When you look at the organization, do you see that the meetings, reports, presentations, and ideas are tools people use or do they seem to be the reason people have jobs in the first place? With this level of management, you really need to ask yourself if you really like this kind of environment; because if you're the type of individual that wants to get things done, this may actually be a very frustrating place to work.

Late Nights, And Work Being Taken Home

For the reasons given above (meetings upon meetings, reports, etc.), many find that they cannot accomplish all their work at work and so they end up taking work home – and it becomes more the rule than the exception. For some, having to do a lot of work at home is a badge of honor and is thought to bode well for their success in the organization.

Still, don't get me wrong: If your organization values hard work and offers appropriate rewards for the value it receives, that is different. If you gain status because you work long hours and this is not tied to a value for the company (client/customer), then you might want to re-evaluate the values this organization is actually promoting.

Group Appreciation – Team of the Quarter/Year

The 3rd epiphany manager values what teams can achieve – and teamwork itself – to the point that it may actually be difficult to be recognized for individual accomplishments. If you look at how you and your team are appreciated and it's all about the team or group, it is a good indication that you are being managed by a 3rd epiphany manager.

It is not uncommon for this type of organization to have the team of the quarter, large boards or banners proclaiming which group or team is meeting or exceeding the latest goals – and it's not necessarily a bad thing. The Japanese have used this kind of organizational philosophy for decades and have successfully taken over the automotive and electronics markets. In many respects, Japanese culture is very much a reflection of 3rd-epiphany-management style and philosophies. They don't seem to have done too poorly in business.

Working in teams can be a good thing, but there are times when it is entirely inappropriate. The Fukushima Nuclear Power Plant disaster is a prime example. With so much dependence on the team and having consensus, critical decisions around environmental safety at the plant were delayed until it was too late. (Report: Japan, utility at fault for response to nuclear disaster, 2011)

Participation Is Documented On Performance Evaluations

It's an interesting phenomenon that as managers progress to the higher epiphanies, the influence those epiphanies have on the organization increases. Usually, 1st epiphany behavior has a relatively small sphere of influence; but by the time 3rd epiphany behavior takes hold, its influence over organizational behavior is far greater. Nonetheless, every organization operates from its core values and beliefs, and participation is one such belief.

Management keeps track of participation in meetings, problem-solving sessions, and other gatherings where a person is expected to contribute for the good of the group. Because 3rd epiphany organizations believe so strongly that participation is crucial to their success, it is also commonly written into their performance evaluation processes. What better way to communicate the importance of participation to the organization than to make it mandatory and a part of everyone's performance evaluation?

Affirmative Action Lives Here

Third-epiphany-managed groups naturally welcome diversity. In fact, diversity is such a highly valued trait of 3rd epiphany managers that, if you are from a minority population or a different culture, you may find great opportunity for advancement in this organization. Affirmative action lives here. Given two people with identical skills and knowledge, this manager will have the tendency to select people from diverse backgrounds or non-traditional career paths. The core belief of this manager is that the more diverse the group, the greater the opportunity for different perspectives and better solutions.

General Motors placed a female psychologist in the plant manager role, Dr. Patricia M. Carrigan. After the Atlanta manufacturing plant, she was made the plant manager at GM's Bay City plant. She was very successful and the plant turned its performance record around from being one of the worst to one of the best in the company. She is credited with saving the plant by gaining union cooperation for cost-cutting and finding new business. (Rogers, 2005)

Respect Makes A Good Place to Work

Listening is one of the greatest forms of appreciation; and in a 3rd-epiphany-managed organization, management is willing to listen. Since everyone has value and can bring value to the organization, everyone is respected for who they are and appreciated for what they bring to the table, so to speak. You can find your voice in these organizations because the 3rd epiphany manager will take the time to listen to what you have to say and they will consider it on face value. The respect accorded each individual makes these types of organizations some of the best places to work.

Size Matters

In smaller organizations, having meetings that include everyone is simple. It's easy to get the word out and get feedback from everyone. Decisions are made rapidly by the group, focus is usually intense, and everyone has personal goals to achieve. As 3rd-epiphany-managed organizations grow, however, getting the word out to everyone and getting feedback (or even giving them the opportunity) can become quite a challenge. More often than not, what took minutes or hours before can become days or weeks as the organization grows.

Responsibilities change within organizations as they grow and those changes affect the dynamic of how decisions are made. In a small organization, there is likely to be one person that is responsible for real estate decisions; but in a larger organization, there may be ten or 11 people that have similar responsibilities. These people will want to evaluate and have input to the decision since the outcome affects them. Keep growing, and there may be representatives across the globe with the same responsibilities, each with an opinion and desired course of action that favors their own situation. As people join the organization in different areas, it becomes more difficult to reach consensus and agreement. It is about this time that people start to wish for the "good old days" when things happened much more quickly.

I witnessed this kind of challenge firsthand while working at Google. When I first started working there, decisions were made quickly in meetings of eight to 12 people. Later on, as the company grew, attendance at meetings swelled to 40 to 60 people across the world and decisions were not made until everyone had their chance to understand and comment on the issue at hand. Meetings went from one hour to four or five hours even though we were dealing with the same types of issues.

Third-epiphany management may become frustrated with the timeliness of decisions by the group; but because they value the diversity of input more, they simply find ways to cope with the delays. You can see why 3rd epiphany organizations start to invest in technology to meet these demands.

Who's got The Ball?

One problem that can plague this type of organization is the proliferation of decisions that come from tackling a single issue. An individual has a single set of values and beliefs they use to compare and contrast possibilities as they come to a decision. Groups, on the other hand, have multiple sets of values and beliefs. And so when a group addresses an issue, what emerges is a spectrum of different methods to evaluate and possible answers to consider – and this can cause considerable delay as the group first decides which criteria and method to use and then what outcome is best.

But aside from the difficulty of getting to a decision, even assigning the task can prove difficult, if not impossible, in a group situation. Issues are often taken up by volunteers that will take actions that favor their interests and the interests of the groups they represent. This may or may not be in the best interest of the organization or company as a whole.

And of even greater concern is the inability to define who is responsible for the outcome. The manager is like a quarterback who throws the ball to the team. And three things can happen when the ball is thrown: Someone in the group can catch the ball and run with it, the ball can just fall to the ground, or it can be picked up by someone from outside the team if the issue is important enough.

But in each situation, the more important question is "Who's got the ball?" When delays or bad decisions occur and the 3rd epiphany manager tries to determine who's got the ball, they usually find that no single person can be identified as the responsible party. Trying to hold a group responsible for delays or bad decisions is difficult at best.

Running things by consensus and group votes can also split organizations into factions that may even work to sabotage the efforts of the group. But a 3rd epiphany manager will have the tendency to drive for consensus and attempt to continue to have meetings until all the issues are resolved – or people give up.

As an aside, it is a common tactic in this type of organization to assign work to those who were not able to attend or were not there to defend their positions. While working in teams and groups can be a great thing, there are many pitfalls if this hard-driven philosophy is taken to the extreme.

We Live and Die Together

Left with no one holding the ball, the 3rd epiphany manager holds the group itself responsible for the outcomes – the live-and-die-together mentality. This can end up being reflected in performance evaluations. Everyone's contributions will be aggregated into the group's, and individual evaluations will reflect the group's performance overall. But the manager sees themselves in this light as well. They identify with the successes and failures of the group and expect their own performance evaluations to reflect this.

Speeches by the 3rd epiphany manager are filled with "we" and "us" and words that identify the group as a team, working and striving together, sharing in the success and challenges. The group's goals and progress toward those goals will be posted for everyone to see. If you have the feeling that you are all in the same boat, you're correct. And the genuine respect and appreciation team members feel from their 3rd epiphany managers is often fondly remembered long after people have moved on to other pursuits.

Project Team of the Month – The Right T-Shirt/Patch/Button

Team identification and esprit de corps will be fostered and supported by 3rd epiphany managers at every turn. Team patches, identification marks, mottos, and other such group identification are prevalent and encouraged. Do you have team shirts, jackets, hats, or such? Is there a team identification banner or patch? These are strong indicators that a 3rd epiphany manager is leading your group.

Typically, 3rd epiphany managers support a project team of the month, and the honor rolls around to each group in the organization. The company bulletin may call out a new team each month for recognition. The key is that all members of the team will at some time be called out and recognized for their effort and contribution. (Remember that each member is seen as equally important in the organization by this manager.)

Third-epiphany-managed organizations are, for the most part, very pleasant places to work. They are characterized by appreciation, diversity, and teamwork. They can also be afflicted with analysis paralysis, groupthink, lack of direction, and other group traits that cause inefficiencies. But overall, the 3rd epiphany organization is heads and shoulders above the other two situations we've described thus far. If you find yourself working in this type of managed organization, you can count your blessings. About 30 percent of the organizations out there have 3rd epiphany managers.

Working for a 3rd Epiphany Manager

Sometimes group-oriented processes make for a frustrating existence in 3rd-epiphany-managed organizations. Decisions may be held up in committee as data is analyzed to the nth degree or the organization may flounder without clear direction as it pursues one idea after the next. But for the most part, the 3rd epiphany manager's genuine respect for people and what they bring to the table makes it a refreshing and pleasant place to work.

As with the 1st and 2nd epiphany managers, you can help this manager on their path to leadership by providing new ideas and opportunities for growth through your actions. One thing that differentiates the 3rd epiphany manager, however, is that they will actually give you the opportunity to express your ideas and try different things. At this level, you may have the luxury to help the manager see different prospects and possibilities as opposed to spending your energy trying to better your work environment as with managers at the beginning stages of leadership.

Your Opinion and Ideas Count

Since 3rd epiphany managers believe that everyone is smarter about something, you can use this as an opportunity to voice your opinions and ideas and be heard. These managers will not only consider your thoughts, they will also bring your opinion to the group so they can offer their opinions and comments.

Take advantage of the opportunity and make your opinions and ideas known when asked. There is no opinion or idea that does not provide some additional perspective or insight. Granted, the opinion or idea may provide more insight about you than the subject being discussed. But in reality, speaking your thoughts does a couple of things: First, it advertises to this manager that you care and are engaged in the business; and, second, it gives you the opportunity to guide the group and manager to new perspectives and possibilities. Some of the best ideas have come from outrageous thoughts, and even whacky ideas can spawn great products and services.

Talk Softly, and Carry Big Ideas

In this type of environment, the people that interject first and talk the loudest normally have the most input and seem to get their way more often. Take a different tack: Compete with inspiration and brilliance instead of with volume. You may have to wait until the discussion dies down and the manager asks for additional comments or ideas, but this is your window of opportunity. Big ideas usually start with a question. So offer an engaging question, and then provide the answer. You don't need to exercise the lungs, just appeal to the minds and hearts of the group.

If you consistently provide great ideas and provoke thought, you will be seen as the go-to person for inspiration and perspective. In this position, you provide an example to the manager that individuals think differently and have different internal processes to come up with great results, which supports their belief that diversity is needed.

Don't Participate in Groupthink

There is a great story about groupthink provided by Jerry B. Harvey in his book *"The Abilene Paradox: The Management of Agreement"* (Harvey, 1974, summer). In this article, he tells the following story:

"On a hot afternoon visiting in Coleman, Texas, the family is comfortably playing dominoes on a porch, until the father-in-law suggests that they take a trip to Abilene [53 miles north] for dinner. The wife says, 'Sounds like a great idea.' The husband, despite having reservations because the drive is long and hot, thinks that his preferences must be out of step with the group and says, 'Sounds good to me. I just hope your mother wants to go.' The mother-in-law then says, 'Of course I want to go. I haven't been to Abilene in a long time.'

"The drive *is* hot, dusty, and long. When they arrive at the cafeteria, the food is as bad as the drive. They arrive back home four hours later, exhausted.

"One of them dishonestly says, 'It was a great trip, wasn't it?' The mother-in-law says that, actually, she would rather have stayed home, but went along since the other three were so enthusiastic. The husband says, 'I wasn't delighted to be doing what we were doing. I only went to satisfy the rest of you.' The wife says, 'I just went along to keep you happy. I would have had to be crazy to want to go out in the heat like that.' The father-in-law then says that he only suggested it because he thought the others might be bored.

"The group sits back, perplexed that they together decided to take a trip which none of them wanted. They each would have preferred to sit comfortably, but did not admit to it when they still had time to enjoy the afternoon."

This a classic example of groupthink where the individuals in the group were making decisions based upon what they perceived others were thinking. You might be tempted to think this quaint example isn't very common or realistic, until you consider that the Bay of Pigs incident in April 1961 was actually precipitated in part by President Kennedy's cabinet exhibiting groupthink characteristics in their flawed decision-making process. The incident cost hundreds of people their lives.

Advocate against groupthink. It's a phenomenon that can have very serious consequences. So what can you do to prevent it? Play devil's advocate and ask the hard questions. Examine all alternatives, and discuss different ideas and suggestions with people outside the group.

Think, then Speak – Don't be Afraid to be Yourself

In one of my blogs, I wrote an article titled "*The Most Important 2 Seconds Of Your Career*." I was attempting to portray that making decisions and going to action without at least a momentary pause to consider what you are going to say or how your actions will be received could actually affect the rest of your life. In the nuclear fields, we talk about taking two seconds to consider the consequences of the actions that you are about to take. I would recommend that you use this same technique before you speak in group meetings.

While passions and energy may be elevated in meetings, take time to consider what you are about to say, but don't be afraid to be yourself. The witty comment that you are considering to spout out may be entirely appropriate, but take two seconds to consider if there are or could be consequences.

Don't Be Afraid To Disagree

In step with discouraging groupthink, don't be afraid to disagree. Don't disagree simply to be contrary; but if you have what you believe is a valid concern, then by all means voice it. Disagreement sometimes leads to a much better outcome and an even better way to solve problems. If you normally agree, then your disagreement will carry more weight as people will recognize it as a deviation from your norm.

Support Your Opinions with Ideas, Data, and the Opinions of Other Great Leaders

Within the context of providing opinions or ideas, do what you used to do in school – provide data or other backup from credible sources. You may not be asked to present the data or backup immediately, but have it ready nonetheless. This advertises the fact that you are ready for meetings, that you know the subject matter and are engaged in the process.

Since many of the situations you address will help decide group direction or behavior (remember that 3rd epiphany managers send many of these issues to the group) it is the perfect opportunity to draw from the experiences of other great leaders. Great leaders that have faced similar situations often inspire others to reach for solutions or realize new perspectives. The Internet has made it so much easier to examine and learn from the lives and actions of great leaders and you can usually adapt their circumstances to support your opinion.

Ask "Is This The Right Thing To Be Doing?"

It's easy to get caught up in the day-to-day aspects of the 3rd-epiphany-managed organization. And it's just as easy for the 3rd epiphany manager to go along with the group. Social influence and the desire for social conformity can cloud our decisions and lead us in directions that may not be in the best interests of the group. Someone in the group needs to ask the larger question, "Are we doing the right thing?" or "Is this how we should respond?" or even "What should we do about this?" This is different than asking "Are we doing it right?"

If you're not seeing the 3rd epiphany manager step back in meetings to ask the larger question of whether the actions being contemplated will take the group in the right direction, it may be time for you to pose the question. By asking this, you set the example for the manager. In reality, it is a question that every leader needs to answer.

Ask What the Organization Should Look Like In Five Years

Leaders have a vision of what they are working toward and what the future should look like. A 3rd epiphany manager may not have articulated a vision yet or even realize that one needs to be articulated in order for the group to be successful. You can help them with this by asking the question, "What do we look like in five or ten years?"

By asking this question, the manager will either start to address the question of vision or defer it until they are ready to discuss it. If they defer it, find a way to bring it up to them in private or at another appropriate moment. It is a touchy question. The reason, as you might expect, is that they won't be prepared to make any off-the-cuff statements declaring their expectations for the future if they haven't really given the subject much thought. If they have considered it but aren't yet able to articulate their vision very precisely, they may be open to the discussion. You may actually have an opportunity to help shape the future of the organization or group in this case. If they can articulate their vision of the future, then you should be able to see how and where everyone in the group can participate to support that direction.

In reality, this is a very important question to ask of any 3rd epiphany manager. So if the question is deferred, wait for a more appropriate time to bring the subject up again – but don't let it go. It needs to be answered for the good of the group. A great, articulated vision of the future can help alleviate uncertainty about the direction of the organization and help people think more constructively about the present and how they can make that future come to pass.

Volunteer To Lead a Group or Activity

"A leader is one who, out of madness or goodness, volunteers to take upon himself the woe of the people. There are few men so foolish, hence the erratic quality of leadership in the world."

John Updike

Volunteer to lead a group or activity. This puts you squarely in the limelight so that the manager can observe how you perform in a leadership role as well as how the group reacts to your behaviors, actions, and words. The experience will also present an opportunity for you and the manager to build a relationship. At the same time, it provides more opportunities for the manager to hone their people skills in different settings.

Volunteering can also open new opportunities for you as you seek to grow or learn about organizations. Even if you never intend to be a manager, the experience will give you further insight into how complex leadership roles are and what it takes to be a successful leader. In either case, the understanding will create a greater bond of appreciation between you and your manager as you both grow and learn.

Ask To Be Mentored By Them

Asking a 3rd epiphany manager to be your mentor raises the stakes for both of you. The manager now must become a teacher. This requires them to study and research leadership and how to do it effectively. This not only opens them up to new learning opportunities, but it also cascades to you. True mentorship requires work for each of you – you have to do the assignments and research; they have to observe, plan, and provide lessons that benefit you (and in many cases, themselves).

True mentorship is difficult at best in a direct employee relationship. Within mentoring, there is an expectation of confidentiality that might not be possible with that relationship. Open, honest dialogue must take place for mentoring to be effective. In this case, you are really looking for some guidance and assistance toward a pre-stated goal. If the manager works in another group, a true mentoring relationship may flourish.

Before asking a manager to be your mentor, make sure that both of you are willing to make the commitment. It will probably require at least weekly meetings for discussion and review. Do you and the manager have one to two hours a week that you can spend reviewing the week and planning the next? If you can do it, a mentoring relationship can do wonders for both the mentor and mentee.

The previous actions are recommendations. Your manager may or may not be responsive or ready to take on the responsibilities, learn about the next steps, or have an open mind that allows them to progress on their journey. It's common for many people to progress to one of these levels and stay there or take years to go through the next epiphany. Your actions and words can help with that, but only if the manager is ready.

Pathways to the 4th Epiphany

If you have identified yourself as a 3rd epiphany manager, you are very likely to be in the upper level of high-performing managers; but like anything in this life, we can always find room to improve. Most 3rd epiphany managers are well liked, known as very respectful, value diversity, and care for all their people. They normally have many years of experience and are starting to move into senior-level positions. They have learned that the more they learn, the more there is to learn.

The Paradox of Change

Change is a part of life, and it's a very important part of the journey to becoming a leader. I have spent years studying the relationship between change and leadership, and I can tell you that they are inexorably tied to each other. At this point in the book I'd like to deviate a little with a discussion about change – both for the manager and the organization. Consider the following quote:

> *"One of the things I learnt when I was negotiating was that until I changed myself I could not change others."*
>
> *Nelson Mandela*

President Mandela realized that, as a leader, he had to change before others would. But what are the implications of that realization or epiphany? Most of us, either in our personal or professional lives, know someone or are acquainted with an organization that would like to change. The change would be beneficial to all parties. A logical or persuasive discussion is pursued, but to no avail. The organization's response is "…just another new program of the week." Individuals respond with

"I've heard that before" or "You're probably right, but...." The final outcome is always the same – nothing.

Organizations and people do change, but why? What happens to get the change started? How is change initiated and sustained? People and organizations are in a constant state of change. Change is in response to a person's or organization's environment. If you want change, change the environment. But here is the paradox: If you want others to change, you must change. The reason is that you are a part of the environment and, if you change, others must adapt to your changes. You, therefore, become the catalyst and the driving force behind changes in the environment and subsequently in others.

"No man is an island..."

John Donne,
Devotions Upon Emergent Occasions

Each of us interacts with many other people through our actions. Even when we try not to interact, we always interact to some degree. For example, if you live the life of a hermit, you still leave behind others who are affected by your absence. From the moment you are born, you start to affect your environment and therefore cause people to tend, feed, and care for you. You become part of the environment that others must contend with and with whom they must relate.

This phenomenon has been studied as a sidelight to change within an organization. An example of this is within the article, *"Be a model leader of change"* by Schneider and Goldwasser. Schneider and Goldwasser state, "Perhaps most importantly, you must set an example – and make sure it's noticed – to implement a change-management plan. Too often employees don't see anything new about the actions of those supposedly leading the initiative, so they assume that this, too, will pass. That's why symbolic acts are so powerful" (Schneider, 1998). This observation supports that the change agent must change in ways that are meaningful to the organization.

In all the articles that I have read about change, every one called for some type of action on the part of the change agent. The change agent is the person with the power to change the environment. Zimmerman evaluated the manager's role in response to change and found that the manager could "...acknowledge the need for change and strive to be its master; or resist change and fall prey to its unrelenting push" (Zimmerman, 1995). This supports the idea that, as the environment changes, so must the manager and organization. Both the environment and the actions of the change agent are interdependent.

Roger Stuart came to the following conclusion: "... on the ground as it were, what managers may actually be managing (or not as the case may be) is their own and others' change journeys originating in a wide variety of personal, secondary triggers to change. Thus, they are working with individual perceptions and responses which, whether voiced or not, represent the actuality of change in organizations" (Stuart, 1995). Stuart's analysis looked at the interpersonal levels in the change process and concluded that change can be evaluated at this level. It is the manager's *change journey* that evokes responses from the organization.

In *"The challenge of perpetual change"* (Sweeney, 2000), a person in a changing environment must "... invest resources in it, lead it, and exploit it." Again, in this case, the person is required to change due to changes in their environment. We all have responses to our environment. If the responses are semi-automatic or automatic, we call these habits.

Because of this interrelationship, we are the environment. For example, if a person who rides with you in your carpool decides to ride his bike instead, this will have an effect on the other members of the carpool. The cost will be split among fewer people, there will be one less stop in the morning and evening, and the conversation will lack their input and ideas. A single person that decides to ride a bike to work instead of riding in the carpool accomplished all this change.

As you can see from the research and by testing this concept yourself, the environment and the change agent are very interdependent. If one changes, the other must change. We are not islands. As it is in physics, our actions cause reactions in our environment. With awareness, a keen sense of the results of our actions, and a clear vision of where you want to go, a person can make changes in themselves that change their environment as they wish. This is actually easier than it seems. The hard part is determining the reactions that would occur for any given situation. Even so, most people have an innate ability to change their behavior to affect their environment and achieve the responses that they desire.

> *"Change is the law of life. And those who look only to the past or present are certain to miss the future."*
>
> *John F. Kennedy*

Now that we see that this journey is really about the changes that we must make within ourselves, here are some activities and actions to help you reach the next realization or epiphany.

Exploring 20/30/50 in Meetings

During my years in management and leadership, I have invoked a number of changes to organizations that have spanned the spectrum from trivial (or so I thought) to complete replacement of the core values of the group. During these changes there seemed to be some of the group that would support the change, some that would fight it, and some that really didn't care. As I continued making changes in organizations, I came to recognize some commonalities of behavior when I implemented a change that affected the core values of the organization.

First, a core value is one that is held deeply and by all. It could be devotion to honesty or to a specific color of paper for a report. It just has to be held deeply and by all involved. My observation was that when I made a change to a core value, 20 percent of the people would support and work to make the change happen, 30 percent of the people would fight it, and 50 percent of the people would go on about their normal business not really caring. Why is this?

This is my personal observation and is by no means a scientific study. I'm not sure why 20 percent would support the change; I just find that about 20 percent of the people simply want change. They, for whatever reason, agree with, believe in, or desire the changes or just want change for the sake of change. These are the people that will help you make the changes happen. Seek them out and empower them.

The 30 percent group is the hardest to deal with. They do what almost everyone does when faced with a difficult situation – they exhibit the primal fight-or-flight reaction. I suspect that the reason they go in to fight-or-flight mode is that the proposed change is contrary to their personal values. Since they are very reluctant to change their core values, they will fight the changes (tooth and nail if they have to). You will see everything from completely ignoring the change (total neglect) to outright sabotage. In any case, these people will leave the organization, either by themselves or by direction. So yes, if you make changes to the core values of an organization, you can expect to lose about 30 percent of your people. The problem is that you cannot always predict which people will fall into this group. It could be your leadership or a majority of your professionals, but it will encompass about 30 percent of the total population.

The 50 percent group is more or less passive about the change. The change doesn't affect or disturb their personal core values very significantly and, therefore, they just go along with the change. They can be vocal, either with their support or dissatisfaction; but they wind up just going along with the change or changes. You can persuade this group by vision, logic, and rewards.

Now that you have this knowledge, how do you use it? Well, *carefully* is my recommendation. If you are going to make changes to processes, programs, priorities, plans, or personnel (the five "Ps"), you will most likely see this split and the accompanying reactions. When you contemplate a change, introduce it as an idea in a meeting and see what the reaction is. Do you see the 20/30/50? Who are in the 20 percent? Who are in the 30 percent? The specific people who comprise these groups can determine if your changes will succeed or not. Is your boss one of the 20, 30, or 50 percent? Can you afford to lose the 30 percent?

Change is never easy; but by recognizing who comprises each group, you can select those changes that have a greater chance of success.

Make Decisions – The Ones That Need To Be Made

It was hot in July and there was no air conditioning. The meetings took place weekly, but this one was different. The leader of the group got up and read a document that he had prepared before the meeting and then asked the group what they should do about it. The group was shocked by the scope of change that was proposed. Of the seven that were there, only two stated that they would support it. The rest either opposed it outright or thought it was not in the best interest of the group. The debate lasted a couple of hours. At the conclusion of the meeting, President Lincoln thanked his cabinet, but had already decided to go forward with the Emancipation Proclamation.

If President Lincoln had followed what the group had recommended, many people would not have the freedom that we all enjoy today – and I suspect that the Civil War would not have gone as it did. Instead, President Lincoln set in motion a new course for a nation and an example for the world.

There are times when a leader must make decisions that are contrary to popular thought at the time. But only by leading can the leader make anything different in the world. I can't tell you when you should make decisions that are not popular, but I can tell you that they will most likely come from the heart or gut and will *feel* like the *right* thing to do. They may not always work out, but only by leading the group into territories that are not currently being explored do we learn and grow.

It's Okay To Make Mistakes. It's How We Learn

Thomas Edison was asked about his many failures in his quest to invent the electric light. His famous answer was, *"I have not failed 10,000 times. I have not failed once. I have succeeded in proving that those 10,000 ways will not work. When I have eliminated the ways that will not work, I will find the way that will work."*

Making mistakes and failing is how we learn – and both you and your people will make mistakes. It's a part of making progress. Find a way to celebrate what you learn from those failures and institutionalize that knowledge so that others can learn from it too. If you know that the probability of mistakes are high, then find a way to protect the operations and processes if a mistake is made.

Tolerance and patience is what is needed when we discover mistakes. Your organization needs to notify you when mistakes are made; and you should not dish out punishment or shoot the messenger, as it were. This will only serve to isolate you from the group and make it more difficult for you to learn of other mistakes when they occur. Your goal should be to find ways to keep communication open and free. You do that by what I said above: Celebrate what you and others have learned.

Sometimes It Is Better To Ask Forgiveness than Permission

In this world, as things spin faster and faster, opportunities sometimes slip us by because of the approval processes we put in place to go after them. Whether internal or external, great opportunities don't come along very often. It pays to be ready so you can take advantage when they do, but this may require that you take action before official approvals can take place.

I had this type of situation occur one time. I was faced with the opportunity to fix a situation for a client that would cause significant expense for us. I knew that it would be literally weeks before I had the approvals and by then I knew the client would most likely have become a former client. I took it upon myself to move ahead with the correction and, in doing so, earned the loyalty of a Fortune 50 client. I was later informed that it was the right decision and earned praise for making things right with the customer while staying within our company values.

Experience has taught me that most leaders face this situation at some point in their careers. There may come a time when you face a similar situation and decision. Be prepared. Consider what could happen and work though the mental exercises of what you would do. What you do with the opportunity is up to you. I recommend that you take whatever action feels right, if it aligns with your company's values and interests.

Ask What Will Make Each of Your People Successful and What Your Role Is In That Process

Every person that works for you has a life plan. They may not be able to articulate it or even be willing to share it with you; but if you ask, they might share some of it. Whether it is to become a famous opera singer or an Olympian, or a great leader in their own right, you need to know what that is. Determine how you can help, within the context of the organization to which you belong. You should take an active role in helping people succeed. After all, isn't that what you were hired to do? What will make them successful in their position? What will make them successful in life? If you can help them in both, you will earn a revered place in their lives (and this sometimes lasts a lifetime).

Meyers-Briggs Type Indicator Assessment

The Meyers-Briggs Type Indicator (MBTI) is an assessment that categorizes people's tendencies into 16 different groups. From this, you can start to understand how some people view the world and the reasons they react the way they do. It is not a predictor of people's behavior in all situations; but if you look at an entire population, it can offer some predictability.

I recommend that you take the MBTI for what you can learn about yourself. It can show you why you have certain tendencies and why you interact with people in certain ways. It can also help you see how similar and different your people are.

Quick Caveat: You cannot determine who will be successful or who would do better in any one situation with it.

There are many books that have been written about the MBTI, and it is a worthwhile study. As a tool, it is useful to help you identify differences and similarities in the traits of people. You may find it fascinating. I certainly did.

Become a Mentor

A mentor, according to *Dictionary.com* is "... a wise and trusted counselor or teacher" or "… an influential senior sponsor or supporter." Having come this far in your journey toward leadership, you should start to give back what others have taught you – and to that end, I highly recommend that you consider becoming a mentor.

I speak more to this in later chapters. It is a learning experience and growth opportunity for both you and the mentee. When done correctly, you will assist someone as they pursue their life's goals and more than likely you will earn a loyal friend for a lifetime. Not a bad return on your investment.

> *"The growth and development of people is the highest calling of leadership."*
>
> Harvey S. Firestone

141

Take Classes to Understand Behavior and Motivation

As a leader, your area of study is human behavior. Whether you came from engineering, marketing, sales, manufacturing, or the arts, you are now a student of human behavior. Your work is with motivation, emotions, goals, communication, training, education, and all the other areas of human interaction and development.

Like most of us, you were probably chosen to be a supervisor or manager because of your abilities as an individual contributor. And having learned more about what leadership is, it may seem silly now that anyone would confuse a person's superior work performance with their ability to lead – but it is still very often the case. We in the U.S. have only recently discovered that choosing leaders on the basis of individual accomplishment is not really advantageous. The typical leadership selection process is not geared to identify the traits and tendencies of leaders, let alone quantify their potential for success. So here we are, many times left to educate ourselves in the art and science of leadership.

I recommend that you take every opportunity to learn about people and how they behave in organizations and groups. Learn about psychology, sociology, and group dynamics. These are the tools in your new trade of leadership. We spend countless hours training our airline pilots and nuclear power plant operators, but spend almost no time training our leaders about how to understand the people that they must lead.

Take a class, read books, talk to others, attend seminars, join online discussions – do whatever you can to increase your knowledge in this area. If you have found a mentor to guide you, they most likely have a number of recommended courses or books for you to read. But never quit learning. We learn new things about people all the time. The leadership craft is always developing new and better ways to lead and inspire. You have already started down that road by reading this book, but it is a course of study that will take a lifetime. Keep going, keep learning, and keep leading.

Study Inspirational and Effective Leaders

Leadership can be learned, and observation and emulation is one of the best ways to learn. The key is to find the right examples of leadership from which to learn. Study the associated behaviors of 4th epiphany leaders and find people that act in that manner. Be sure to look at the organizational reflective behaviors to validate that the person that you are learning from is actually a 4th epiphany leader.

These people exemplify 4th epiphany leadership: Nelson Mandela, Ronald Reagan, Abraham Lincoln, and Margaret Thatcher. They each had their own personal road to leadership and were not born 4th epiphany leaders. They learned how to lead as they encountered different situations in their lives. We recognize 4th epiphany behavior at their high points, but few of us witnessed their journey to become 4th epiphany leaders. There are others: Steve Jobs, Gandhi, Warren Buffett, Herb Kelleher, etc. One could even be your current leader. About 5 percent of those in leadership roles are truly 4th epiphany leaders.

Pay specific attention to how they get things done. This is the crux of what leaders do – accomplish things. Learn how they inspired people and gained fanatical loyalty. When you gain the hearts and minds of people, you can accomplish great things that will last beyond your direct influence, and this leads us to the next subject.

Heart and Mind

Leadership is about engaging the hearts and minds of people. You can tell people what to do and, because of your position of power, they will do what you ask. But, at best, that only engages the body, not the soul. If you want to have an organization that performs above and beyond, you need to find a way to inspire them. You need to engage their hearts.

Napoleon understood this when he said, "A soldier will fight long and hard for a bit of colored ribbon." He understood that the "bit of colored ribbon" represented a cause, position of honor, or recognition of deeds and bravery. A cause can be very powerful motivation for some; and while most leaders will never ask their followers to give their lives for the cause, they can inspire people to the point that they will do almost anything to support the cause or gain recognition for their effort.

Devotion to the cause is a double-edged sword, though. On the one hand, people can be so inspired and motivated that they will find a way to achieve the goal. On the other hand, this level of motivation can cause some to disregard their values and behaviors to go beyond what is acceptable. Leaders need to provide the example and be very clear as to what acceptable behavior is.

So how do you gain their hearts and minds? One way is to articulate an inspiring vision of the future; another is to align your mission with an inspiring cause. As a side note, the promise of riches can be a great motivator, but provides temporary motivation at best. Let's look at some of the situations that inspired groups and people over the years.

For Nelson Mandela, it was to show his country that a better way of life could exist if people were treated as equals and unfair government practices were eliminated. For Steve Jobs and

Apple, it was to create things that enhanced our creative process, were easy to use (they worked with human nature), and were cool.

How do you inspire people when you have an accounting function? What do you do if your job is maintenance of the plant or if you're responsible for waste collection for a small city? While these activities may not seem likely to inspire historical efforts and results, people nevertheless are naturally motivated to do the best that they can. You can use this to make jobs into causes that reflect grand ideals and a path to creativity.

When I was responsible for a maintenance group, our job was to make sure that the plant's equipment operated and was well maintained. On the face of it, how excited can you get over replacing filters and fan belts? Describing it in those terms, you would have difficulty getting people to even apply for the job much less to engage their hearts and minds to accomplish incredible results. The first thing I did was to create a different perspective with which to view our job. We now provided "Professional, effective, and efficient facilities operations, services, and improvements" instead of facilities maintenance. While it may seem like semantics, it is designed to create a vision of what we need to be, how we are supposed to act, and what we are to do. Which would you rather be part of – garbage collections or "North America's leading provider of integrated environmental solutions"? (Waste Management, Inc.)

Visions of the future can provide very powerful motivation and should be crafted to inspire hope and esprit de corps. Create a vision through a well-crafted mission statement, associated goals, and your behavior as the example of what the organization could and should be. If you are successful in engaging people's hearts and minds, then your organization will be well on its way to becoming something that everyone associated with it can be proud of.

Explore Leadership Actions and Group Reactions

As the leader, your actions are directly reflected in the behavior of the group. Taking this into account, try different things. I recommend that you explore how your behaviors are reflected within the group. See what happens when you take the time to pick up trash in one of your areas of responsibility, wear different clothing (a suit or jeans), or make a decision openly in front of the group to show them your priorities. You probably know what reactions you can expect to get when you change your behavior, but validate your assumptions. You might be surprised.

Understand Your Motivation for Becoming a Leader

Why do you want to be a leader? What drives you? Is it the excitement of being the one in-charge, or being seen as one whose opinion counts, or do you like to teach people? There is actually no incorrect answer. What drives you is what drives you. Your internal motivations can last a lifetime or they can be short-term goals.

It's important that you understand your motivation at this point because the next epiphany includes the realization that leadership is a calling and lifelong pursuit. I use the word "calling" because leadership takes over your life and becomes all that you do. A leader is a leader all the time, not just at work or at company functions. They rise to the occasion during church meetings, Boy Scout meetings, the PTA, and pretty much any situation they face – and this includes their family life too.

Being a 3rd epiphany manager will more than likely put you in the upper 25 percent of managers, but only those truly dedicated to the craft of leadership (and essentially the human condition) lead us into the uncharted territory of human endeavors. Not everyone makes it, but I believe that most people have the capacity to become great leaders. There is also the matter of other, more environmental factors that can play a role in leadership – timing and luck seem to play their parts. Being in the right place at the right time is sometimes critical; but unless you know what to do when you get there, the moment will pass you by. Again, leaders are leaders all the time, so when the place and time align, true leaders are ready.

For most of us, several opportunities for leadership will occur in our lifetimes. Will you be ready? That is up to you. Do you have the motivation to live the rest of your life as a leader, to be an example to others, never taking any time off from the role you have accepted? It is a huge commitment that can pay glorious rewards at times. But more often than not, satisfaction comes in the small, everyday wins – the progress toward the cause, the improvement in peoples' lives, or at least the opportunity for it.

An Inflection Point

This journey of epiphanies has brought you to an inflection point – the mathematical description of the point at which a curve changes direction. Beyond this point, the next epiphany will change your perspective and, in some ways, turn your world upside down. Leaders that move forward into the 4th epiphany live with a strange duality of purpose – commitment to leadership as well as to their vision or cause.

Most leaders at this level have dedicated a lifetime to leadership in the obtainment of their visions. They have become part of the 5 percent that change the world – Abraham Lincoln, Henry Ford, Herb Kelleher, Nelson Mandela, Ronald Reagan,

John Kennedy, Martin Luther King, Jr., and Steve Jobs. It's not a bad group to be in, if you choose to be.

"The world as we have created it is a process of our thinking. It cannot be changed without changing our thinking."

Albert Einstein

Chapter 5

The 4th Epiphany

The 4th epiphany leaders are the *crazy ones*, the round pegs in the square holes, the perfectionists, slave drivers, saints, and the devil all in one. They believe that they can change the world – and are the people who do. While 3rd epiphany managers may be very easy to work for and their organizations very nice places to work, working for a 4th epiphany leader is almost never easy. South Africa's President Nelson Mandela gives some insight to the way they think. When asked about his greatest weakness, he is said to have replied that he expects the best of all those with whom he comes in contact, including his most intransigent enemies.

Put a 4th epiphany leader among workers digging in a ditch and ask them what they are doing. The workers are more than likely to answer, "We are digging a ditch. Can't you see that?" Whereas the 4th epiphany leader will answer, "I am building a great cathedral to the glory of God." They have vision, they have passion, and they know how to get where they are going. They make things happen, and they inspire people to get things done.

Fourth epiphany leaders have a different perspective. Those that know them may say they live in a different dimension, on a different planet, in an alternate reality; but if you ask them, they will gladly describe the future they see. And you may find their manner to be so infectious and inspiring that you actually pick up a shovel and start digging in the ditch next to them.

When you showed Steve Jobs something new, more often than not he would ask, "What can you do with it?" when the rest of us were asking, "What is it?" Vince Lombardi didn't look for the best players; he looked for those with the most passion for the game. Talk about a different perspective and vision, Billy Beane, general manager of the Oakland A's baseball team, was being out-spent on every front for the best baseball players. He turned to the statistical sciences to determine who the best players really were. The outcome was a team that won when the experts knew they couldn't. His revelations and methods fundamentally changed how the game of baseball is managed and teams are built. Fourth epiphany leaders change the game.

Fourth epiphany leaders are about permanence. This is one of the first paradoxes that you will notice about them. They long to build or develop things that will last, when all the while they are constantly driving change. Vince Lombardi was always changing his plays and methods, but behind that was the never-changing value that perfect practice makes perfect play on the field on game day. Steve Jobs said, "Being the richest man in the cemetery doesn't matter to me. Going to bed at night saying we've done something wonderful, that's what matters to me." For these 4th epiphany leaders, it's about making a difference and leaving the world a better place because of what they do.

One of the scenes in the movie *"Remember the Titans"* (2000, Disney/Bruckheimer) actually shows a 4th epiphany moment unfold. Set in the South in 1971, Coach Boone had called for his racially divided team to undergo three-a-day football practices until the players could learn to get along and respect each other. To that end, they were also required to learn something about the players of the other race. Gerry, the white defensive team captain, accuses Julius, one of the black teammates, of deliberately wasting his talents and not playing for the team or him. Julius responds:

Julius: Why should I give a hoot about you? Huh? Or anyone else out there? You wanna talk about the ways? You're the captain?

Gerry: Right.

Julius: You got a job?

Gerry: I've got a job.

Julius: You been doing your job?

Gerry: I've been doing my job.

Julius: Then why don't you tell your white buddies to block for Rev (black quarterback) better? Because they have not blocked for him worth a blood nickel, and you know it! Nobody plays. Yourself included. I'm supposed to wear myself out for the team? What team? Nah, nah. What I'm gonna do is look out for myself and I'ma get mine.

Gerry: See man, that's the worst attitude I ever heard.

Julius: Attitude reflects leadership, Captain.

The words are like a revelation to Gerry, making him realize it is his own attitude and actions that set the wrong example for the team. As he thinks through Julius's comment, Gerry decides to change his behavior to cause the team to think differently. And in the next scene, you see that his new behavior inspires a shift in the culture. When he tackles an offensive player very aggressively during the practice, others on the defense follow suit. He taunts one of the offensive players for not doing his job and this new attitude reverberates within the defensive team. Gerry has become the leader that he needs to be, providing inspiration and setting the culture of doing your best for the team.

This example of leading and reinforcement of a team culture goes beyond the field when later in the movie Gerry is injured in a car accident and is in the hospital. Julius is going to visit him and a nurse stops him.

Nurse: Only kin's allowed in here.

Gerry: Alice, are you blind? Don't you see the family resemblance?   That's   my   brother. (The nurse then lets Julius into the room.)

Though Gerry's injury prevented him from ever playing with the team again, his leadership example continued to inspire the team to reach his vision of winning the state championship. In reality, the changes Gerry brought to the culture of the team lasted well beyond his direct interaction with the team. And so it is with 4th epiphany leadership – leadership at this level is a lifetime endeavor to inspire change that lasts.

So what realization could be so powerful as to change someone into an inspirational leader? In fact, it is a deceptively simple yet extremely complex revelation that has far-reaching consequences.

The 4th Epiphany

It is my job to help my people be successful.

It sounds simple enough. But take a moment to examine it, and the complexities, consequences, and implications become apparent. Let's start with what people need to be successful.

- *Motivation*

Why do people devote themselves to a task or vision? What drives them to succeed? Only when people become engaged in heart and mind do they dedicate body and spirit to the task and vision. And that is precisely where 4th epiphany leaders make a real difference. These leaders are experts at shaping perceptions and creating a vision that inspires and provides the motivation for success.

- *Skill*

As 4th epiphany leaders press into uncharted territory, people often need to develop new skill sets in order to reach the vision. The capabilities to do the task requested are sometimes learned or acquired on the fly because, like *"Star Trek,"* the 4th epiphany leader will truly take their people *"… where no man has gone before."*

- *Knowledge*

An understanding of the process, science, or operation that supports the endeavor is also necessary for people to be successful. Again, it may be that this knowledge is learned as the task is accomplished, with new insights taking place at every attempt. Fourth epiphany leaders fail fast and learn at an incredible rate, bringing everyone along for the ride.

- *Planning or Direction*

While having a vision is good, people must also have a plan or at least a direction so that they can successfully focus their effort. Knowing that you are building a great cathedral is good, but it is also important to know that you start with the foundation. Many 4th epiphany leaders can naturally architect these plans, but most find great people who have a passion for planning and executing.

- *Goals*

People need goals to be successful. Goals provide the needed process or benchmark by which people can be appreciated for their efforts. Goals are a vital part of satisfying the human need to be appreciated, which is what allows them to be successful. Fourth epiphany leaders ensure that goals are provided and that those goals will lead people in the right direction.

- *Priorities*

Even with the vision, plan/direction, and goals, priorities must be articulated and known by all in the organization for it to be successful. Without priorities, tasks may be done out of sequence or resources used to accomplish tasks of marginal value. Priorities also allow groups within the organization that compete for resources to make informed decisions around who gets those resources. Fourth epiphany leaders show their priorities by what they say and do. Many use open-decision-making processes to help followers understand their thought process and priorities.

- *Resources*

All the vision, planning, and good intentions can do nothing without resources. Whether it is hard resources such as cash or materials, or soft resources such as brain power and time, people need resources in order to accomplish the tasks that allow them to reach their goals and vision. Fourth epiphany leaders seem to be very good at resource utilization; they get more out of people and materials than would seem possible. This phenomenon is largely due to the 4th epiphany leader's ability to utilize so much of each person because they have captured their hearts and minds in pursuit of the endeavor.

Of all these requirements, 4th epiphany leaders excel at inspiring people to go above and beyond (motivation). The 4th epiphany leader can touch the hearts and minds of people through the articulation of a compelling vision of the future, clearly stated and well-defined values that appeal to the masses and the ability to weave these into a cause which unites and compels people to join in. Consider this leader's grasp of the vision and where we as a society must go.

> *"I have a dream that my four little children will one day live in a nation where they will not be judged by the color of their skin, but by the content of their character."*
>
> *Martin Luther King, Jr.*

In one sentence, Dr. King provides a vision of equal justice for a nation and ties the values of family, love, and hope to that vision. The imagery of the mind may be different for each of us, but the outcome is consistent. We directly relate, agree, and hope for the same. We are inspired by the compelling future vision and we follow what our hearts and minds desire. The 4th epiphany leader knows this and crafts their message to point us in a direction with a call to action. Dr. King was a master at this. I'm not sure whether he understood it in this context, but he innately understood from his life's experiences how human nature worked and how to use it to accomplish his vision.

Fourth epiphany leaders become masters of communication. A great example is President Ronald Reagan, often referred to as "The Great Communicator." President Reagan had the ability to speak to millions personally. How did he do this? He found a way to discuss complex topics in terms that everyone could relate to and understand. He tied the topics to widely held values that people care about – but most of all, he was sincere. Whenever I would listen to his speeches, it always felt as if he was speaking directly to me, as an old friend. Of course his demeanor was friendly, but he could reach people because he made it clear that he shared the values that were important to them. His sincerity made his passion and belief in his message all the more compelling. They were messages that we can do better, that the future could be brighter, that we can overcome any obstacle, that we can choose to become the best of what humanity can become and that it was our obligation to do so. He believed in us and, in return, we believed in him.

Fourth epiphany leaders understand that to be successful they need to build a relationship with their followers based upon commonly held values and a vision of hope and mutual appreciation. This relationship is what allows trust in the leader's vision to grow and develop. As we evaluate the leader's words and actions, we either validate their actions as supportive of the vision or we become disenchanted due to apparent inconsistencies. President Clinton found this out, as some of his actions and subsequent difficulties during his presidency called into question his commitment to some of the nation's values which prevented him from reaching and working on his future vision for the nation. Sincere belief and supporting actions of true 4th epiphany leaders create tremendous trust and devotion to the cause or vision.

Fourth epiphany leaders hold the perspective that they are there to help. Former Secretary and Chairman of the Joint Chiefs of Staff Colin Powell made the following observation:

> *"Leadership is solving problems. The day soldiers stop bringing you their problems is the day you have stopped leading them. They have either lost confidence that you can help or concluded you do not care. Either case is a failure of leadership."*

Fourth epiphany leaders will do what it takes to help people be successful. Whether it is reconsidering a corporate-wide policy or assisting with a copy machine, they will help. The philosophy of most 4th epiphany leaders, however, is to help you learn so you can help yourself in the future. They commonly do not suffer fools long. If you are not willing to help yourself or learn, they typically will not have time for you. On the other hand, if you are willing to try and are passionate about the common cause, they will do whatever is necessary to help you succeed.

Normally, leaders at this level have developed an entire spectrum of techniques and processes over their lives or careers that help them inspire and gain the best from people and organizations. The following are some of the more common 4th epiphany behaviors.

Behavioral Traits of the 4th Epiphany Leader

"Fit no stereotypes. Don't chase the latest management fads. The situation dictates which approach best accomplishes the team's mission."

Colin Powell

In this book, I try to identify some commonalities in the way managers and leaders behave; but because 4th epiphany leaders need to operate as the situation dictates, it becomes more difficult to list a definitive set of behaviors that represent 4th epiphany behavior. So let me preface this section with the disclaimer that these are only some of the many behaviors I have observed which I believe can indicate that a person is operating at the 4th epiphany level. Moreover, simply because a person operates at the 4th epiphany level does not guarantee that the person will be or is a great leader. However, I can say that they have the greatest potential to be one.

Consider a person who can run the 100 meters in 9.3 seconds (current world record is 9.58) but, because of their situation, country of origin, family situation, economic situation, or other factors, they are never given the chance to run in competition. In fact, most people in this world have no idea how fast they can run the 100 meters. You may be a 4th-epiphany-level person who has never had the opportunity to lead due to your situation; but like the runner, you will be ready when called upon.

The Chameleon

Many researchers and scholars of leadership have found it very difficult, if not impossible, to quantify similarities in great leaders. In pursuit of finding the unique set of traits that would guarantee success as a leader, environmental influences such as schooling, race, culture, and upbringing have been studied -- even cranium size and height and more have been examined. They hoped to identify people that had great potential or a group of behaviors that could be taught or learned.

What commonalities were found? None, actually. In reality, behaviors are just the tools that great leaders use to inspire people. The real indicators of leadership are their understanding of human nature and how their behavior affects perceptions and beliefs.

One problem with identifying a specific group of behaviors for great leaders is that they are chameleons when it comes to behavior. They know how to and will exhibit the behavior that is required to help their organization be successful. That's not to say that they don't have deeply rooted values that drive their behavior, but, rather, they use their behavior in very sincere ways to help and inspire the organization. They can go from being one of the most demanding and animated people you know to being a concerned, quiet listener all based upon what the organization or person needs. So when you look at a 4th epiphany leader, what you find is that they are fluid and willing to change as necessary.

Understands That Constant Change is Normal

"Change is the law of life. And those who look only to the past or present are certain to miss the future."

John F. Kennedy

Fourth epiphany leaders understand that life is change. They realize that we change every day – sometimes imperceptibly, other times dramatically. They like change. In fact, they thrive on it. They appreciate that change is the only way they move forward and that it is not only inevitable, it is necessary for survival and attainment of the vision. After all, as W. Edward Deming said, "It is not necessary to change. Survival is not mandatory."

Consequently, 4th epiphany leaders are the catalysts that drive change in organizations, and they have a sense of urgency and impatience about it. Bring up a cool idea to a 4th epiphany leader and you may find that you are starting a new company or traveling to South America the next day to implement it. You might be surprised at just how fast they can make things happen if it supports their vision and goals.

As stated in Apple's ad *"Think Different,"* these leaders have no respect for the status quo or, for that matter, traditions, beliefs, or public opinion. A person who is heard to say "That's the way we've always done it" is likely to be gone the very next day. Fourth epiphany leaders will be the first to tear down the edifices they just built if doing so would enable them to reach their goals or vision for the future faster.

Drives Change around Consistent Values

Change isn't made for the sake of change, however. Paradoxically, at the core of the 4th epiphany change-tornados are values that never change – values such as service to humanity, respect for nature, beliefs in individual rights and freedom, and that anything can be improved upon. They live with fires in their bellies, but there is always an unchanging principle, the rock upon which they stand, that drives consistency in the way they look at the world and make decisions.

One such 4th epiphany leader, Herb Kelleher, would try almost anything as long as the employees came first, and that included NEVER laying off anyone. This is reflected in many of his speeches, actions, and quotes, but it goes far deeper than that.

We hear many company leaders say that employees come first, but how many say, "A company is stronger if it is bound by love rather than by fear"? I'm not sure how many CEO's have the value of loving their employees; but Herb did, and they saw it in his actions every day. Here's what the employees of Southwest Airlines did in response to that unchanging value:

On Boss's Day, October 14, 1994 the employees of Southwest Airlines bought and paid for this ad in "*USA Today.*"

"Thanks Herb,

"For remembering every one of our names.
"For supporting the Ronald McDonald House.
"For helping load baggage on Thanksgiving.
"For giving everyone a kiss (and we mean everyone).
"For listening.
"For running the only profitable major airline.
"For singing at our holiday party.
"For singing only once a year.
"For letting us wear shorts and sneakers to work.
"For golfing at the LUV Classic with only one club.
"For outtalking Sam Donaldson.
"For riding your Harley Davidson into Southwest Headquarters.
"For being a friend, not just a boss.

"Happy Boss's Day from Each One of Your 16,000 Employees."

As you can see, 4th epiphany leaders will do almost anything to help people be successful, except change their values. And if you think this was a one-time thing, it happened again, in May of 2008, this time by the Southwest Airline Pilots

Association (the same union organization that was picketing American Airlines at the time). In a full page ad in *"USA Today"*:

> "THANK YOU, HERB!
>
> *"From cocktail napkin to cockpit, Herb Kelleher paved the way for the most spirited Company in airline history.*
>
> *"As you step down from the SWA Board of Directors, the pilots of Southwest Airlines would like to thank you, Herb, for 38 years of positively outrageous service to our Company and our pilots. It has been an honor and a privilege.*
>
> *"Southwest Airline Pilots Association"*

Fourth epiphany leaders can develop an almost cult-like following in the process of creating amazing organizations, but it starts with unchanging values. Other 4th epiphany leaders may not have loved their employees as Herb Kelleher did, but their values are just as deeply rooted. Take Steve Jobs's passion for excellence. His relentless quest to improve user experience and to provide simple elegance in technology reshaped the world we live in. At times, those who worked with him called him a megalomaniac for this. Imagine being asked, "What have you done that is wonderful today and what are you going to do tomorrow?" *every day*. Steve's values drove Apple to be one of the most innovative and valued companies in the world. Unchanging values, one of the hallmarks of the 4th epiphany leader.

Can Articulate a Well-defined Mission and Goals at Any Time – And Does

> *"Obstacles are those frightful things you see when you take your eyes off the goal."*
>
> *Henry Ford*

The 4th epiphany leader is the evangelist of dreams and visions of the future. They have an amazing ability to put those visions into a form that has personal meaning for a large audience. This ability to make the mission and goals personal speaks directly to our hearts and minds and, when the vision is compelling to us, we join the cause.

Fourth epiphany leaders are ready to discuss their visions with you anytime, anywhere. Whether you find yourself sitting next to them on an airplane, at a shareholders meeting, or even at their own daughter's wedding, they will find the opportunity to inspire you or at least educate you on their mission. They seem to have boundless energy when you are discussing what animates them.

Every 4th epiphany leader that I have ever met has so completely intertwined their life and mission that it's hard to separate one from the other. The mission becomes them and they become the mission. This phenomenon is infectious, and many people have been evangelized by this leader's dedication, unwavering values, compelling message, and vision for the future.

> *"What you get by achieving your goals is not as important as what you become by achieving your goals."*
>
> *Zig Ziglar*

Paradoxes

We live in a universe of paradoxes. And as mysterious as they can seem, they are really just situations where we don't understand what we are observing as compared to the body of knowledge we have. The mechanisms of action are unknown, hidden from us behind the curtain, as it were. There is a direct connection, but we don't understand it because the *why* is not apparent.

We see paradoxes in all fields of study. But when we explore 4th epiphany leadership, we find that 4th epiphany leaders are quite comfortable amid the paradoxes of life. In fact, paradoxes are associated with their modus operandi. That's why when others were asking what it was; Steve Jobs was already asking what it can do. The 4th epiphany leader doesn't wait to understand the mechanisms but accepts and works with the observations.

Step back to watch a 4th epiphany leader over time and you begin to realize that their lives appear to be filled with paradoxes. They stand for one thing and drive something that seems to be the exact opposite. Here are some of the paradoxes I have identified and you may, too, when you observe them.

- *Flexible And Unwavering*

One paradox common to 4th epiphany leaders is they seem to have infinite flexibility as they work to reach their goals and mission; but this flexibility is directed, not limited, by a very inflexible framework or structure of values and their vision. Mahatma Gandhi, for example, who exemplified pacifism and nonviolence, could be flexible within his extremely rigid framework of values.

"It is better to be violent, if there is violence in our hearts, than to put on the cloak of nonviolence to cover impotence."

Mahatma Gandhi

Before all the Gandhi supporters and scholars fill my email, I understand that this quote in no way actually supports violence. It does speak to being true to one's heart; but as you can see, even within Gandhi's rigid values, there are priorities that allow for flexibility.

President Reagan called the Soviet Union "The Evil Empire," and yet even amid all the rhetoric and his public position, he remained flexible and was willing to change that perception to work with the Soviets for the cause of world peace. In the end, President Reagan forged a relationship with the Soviet Union that changed this former enemy into an ally.

In another example, legendary UCLA basketball coach John Wooden led UCLA to ten NCAA championships in 12 years and was elected to the hall of fame. He is famous for his "Pyramid of Success," a book and philosophy about the building blocks of success in basketball and in life. One of his maxims was *"Flexibility is the key to stability."* Coach Wooden knew the keys to success, as his record so undeniably shows.

- *Perfection Is The Standard; Failing Is Expected*

Tom Peters likes to talk about the constant drive to improve and the never-ending drive toward perfection, as if one could ever get there. Tom impresses upon us his attitude about how to improve as *"Test fast, fail fast, adjust fast."*

The 4th epiphany leader understands that there is no progress unless there is learning and that learning is accomplished by trial and error. They build cultural environments where experimentation is expected and praised. They applaud the good effort and reward great efforts, regardless of their outcome. They admire and appreciate those who, in the relentless effort to obtain the vision, try things. They support people who act, who try, who attempt to push the boundaries of knowledge and the human experience. They also appreciate the fact that the meaning of being human is that we experience failure. They expect that failure will occur and even plan for it.

- *Little Things Matter/Large Objective Focus*

In the blink of an eye or within the same sentence the 4th epiphany leader can go from the big picture to the smallest detail. Remember that the vision is perfection or excellence, but the "devil is in the details."

> *"It's the little details that are vital. Little things make big things happen."*

> *John Wooden*

Fourth epiphany leaders can seem to get mired down in the details from time to time, but it's because they understand that sometimes details are the only thing that stands between them and success. They sweat the small stuff. Steve Jobs was obsessed with the perception of Apple. He personally approved every ad, he complained to Google that the yellow color in their logo didn't look quite right on the iPhone, and he picked the caterer for the Apple cafeteria. In this sense, 4th epiphany leaders can lapse into being micromanagers again. As I said, they may not be the easiest leaders to work for.

The 4th epiphany leader might take several days to decide the location of a button on a new cell phone design or weeks to decide if a website should be 12 or 14 pica font size but can decide the fate of the nation in less than a minute. In 1995, President Nelson Mandela chose to wear the colors of the South African rugby team (the Springboks) during the World Cup championships. In the past, the team colors had come to represent apartheid in the minds of many. But President Mandela knew that if South Africa was to have a chance of becoming one country it must learn to forgive and put aside its old prejudices, from both sides. This seemingly small but courageous act caused a nation to finally come together as one South Africa and started the healing of a country struggling with decades of race issues.

As President Mandela prepared to hand over the cup to the team's captain, he said the following: "François, thank you for what you have done for our country."

And François Pienaar, with extraordinary presence of mind, replied: "No, Mr. President. Thank you for what you have done."

Many people in the world point to this moment with pride as the moment in which South Africa finally became one country and apartheid was no more. By tending to the small detail of wearing a shirt, President Mandela accomplished the much larger vision.

Paradoxes are very common in the universe of the 4th epiphany leader. I can guarantee you that if there are no paradoxes, then you are not dealing with a 4th epiphany leader.

The Example, Never the Exception

Fourth epiphany leaders understand the nature of humans within organizations and realize that they are constantly under the microscope of the people they lead. It is all very normal behavior for people to think that "If it's okay for the boss, it should be okay for me." So 4th epiphany leaders spend time on the things they see as vital to the success of their organization and look for ways to set the example. They recognize that something as simple as bending over to pick up a piece of trash in the lobby can reverberate through an organization. Therefore, they are very particular about their behavior knowing that when they do something, their people will follow suit. If they are demanding in their quest for excellence, their organization will reflect that. If they are lackadaisical about following finances, the organization will adopt the same attitude.

There is never a day off from being a leader because their behavior must consistently reflect the values that reach the goal. Their values drive them to be the example; and their values don't change – and so it is with their behavior.

The Babe Ruth School of Success

While I understand that The Babe never ran a school, in some measure, he taught us about how to achieve success. He had 8,399 times at bat and he struck out 1,330 times, but we remember him for the 714 homeruns he hit. If you look at the numbers, his homerun percentage is only about 8.5 percent. But for something that he did less than 10 percent of the time, he made all the difference.

Fourth epiphany leaders understand this phenomenon and try stuff – lots of stuff. They understand that it's a numbers game. He who tries the most things has the greatest chance to be successful. The 4th epiphany leader may be considered a serial entrepreneur or endless experimenter. It may be said that they are never satisfied, are persistent, or a megalomaniac. But if your leader is endlessly trying new things in the quest of their vision, it's a good sign that you are dealing with a 4th epiphany leader.

Leadership: A Calling and a Profession

It is rare that people are thrust into positions of leadership and become 4th epiphany leaders. They normally feel *called* to the profession and develop into 4th epiphany leaders after years of experience and learning. Most 4th epiphany leaders breathe, drink, and constantly learn about leadership and their causes. To many of them, learning leadership is a means to an end. Either through formal study or life's situations, they experience the epiphanies that open their minds and eyes to truths about human nature that allow them to become effective leaders.

These individuals are proactive to the situations they experience, which means that they have usually already considered most situations that they may face and have predetermined a course of action. Being human, they know that they don't know everything and so they constantly try to add to the breadth and depth of their knowledge and skills when it comes to leadership. This epiphany that their job is to help people succeed extends to their personal lives as well.

Most 4th epiphany leaders understand the tremendous trust and power that comes with the positions they occupy. But interestingly, this realization manifests as fuel that drives their pursuit of the vision and gives them the power to change as they need to.

Natural Teachers

Fourth epiphany leaders are natural teachers. The first thing they usually teach is about their vision and their quest to reach it. Next, they will most likely teach about their values and why they believe in them. It is not uncommon that meetings with a 4th epiphany leader turn into history lessons, discussions on the latest physics behind the technology trends, or a treatise on motivation and appreciation. They recognize that people need knowledge to help them reach their goals and so they use their natural abilities to provide it to them, if they can.

They have learned the gift of putting ideas and philosophies into vivid mental images that are easy to relate to and understand, a gift every teacher would love to have. This is a required skill for them as they must be effective in articulating the vision and goals in terms that are personal to the members of the organization or general population. Mix into this a dash of ego, and you get leaders that love to profess and explain their views on pretty much anything that supports their passions.

Learns From the Past but Doesn't Relive It

At one time, every 4th epiphany leader was a 1st, 2nd, and 3rd epiphany manager. We progress though the epiphanies learning and changing our behavior as we go, but life is not always a straight line or simple progression. There are times we make mistakes and revert back to more familiar behaviors when things are not going our way. We are dealing with humans here and, like all humans, 4th epiphany leaders can lapse and make errors in judgment.

The difference with a 4th epiphany leader is that they get back up on the proverbial horse and continue on. They learn from the past and don't make the same mistakes twice. They are not very tolerant of people who do not learn from their mistakes. They expect of you what they expect of themselves. So an honest mistake will most likely not get you fired, but making the same ones over again will. After all, they want you to succeed and they understand that mistakes happen.

Expects the Best and Accepts Nothing Less

As I mentioned earlier in the chapter, Nelson Mandela stated that his greatest weakness is that he expects the best from everyone, including his enemies. This is a common trait of all 4th epiphany leaders. If you have the opportunity to work for one, you will be tasked with perfection – well, the pursuit of excellence anyway.

Earlier in my career, I had the honor to work in an organization that was led by one of the toughest SOBs and most intelligent visionaries that our country has ever known. Adm. Hyman G. Rickover created the nuclear power program in the U.S. Navy and was a major force in creating our commercial nuclear power program. His relentless drive for safety and operational excellence was only exceeded by the level of professionalism he set for the people that were lucky enough to make it into his programs. In the schools he set up for his programs, it didn't matter if you were in the top of your class or struggling to make the passing grade. You worked hard either way. The school was set up to challenge everyone and did constantly. Adm. Rickover himself demanded the best from everyone that he met or worked for, including himself.

This is another reason I say that 4th epiphany leaders are not easy to work for. They can be some of the toughest bosses that you will ever encounter. Many find working with them too difficult and usually leave for a different situation. If you can find a way to live up to their expectations and stay with them, my bet is that you will be amazed at what the organization will accomplish.

Unquenchable Curiosity

Fourth epiphany leaders have an almost unquenchable curiosity. It is not uncommon for them to read the equivalent of 100-200 pages a night. Sleep gets in the way of discovery and exploration. This will be passed on to the organization in the form of constant research projects and inquiries. If your organization's R&D is huge, it could be a sign that you are working for a 4th epiphany leader.

It would not be uncommon for the 4th epiphany leader to ask to understand how an operator actually uses a machine for their job, with the leader actually taking the time for the operator to teach them. Driven by the need to constantly improve, they gain insight into their operations in this way. So don't be surprised when you find them operating a forklift or packaging machine some day.

Fourth epiphany leaders are the ones that are the most likely to take vacations to destinations that provide enlightenment. They will travel to Asia on vacation to learn about the culture and possible markets or take a trip to South America to explore the mountains while they learn about the transportation and power infrastructure. You find them going to parent/teacher meetings at their children's school so they can explore the training aids, library books, and science labs. You might even find them in the school computer lab trying their hand at programming. They love to learn and it shows.

Finds Wonder in Simple Things and All People

Along with the need to explore and learn, they find wonder in simple things. Fourth epiphany leaders have the ability to turn complexity into simplicity. They also do this for themselves and it manifests itself as finding wonder in everything. They see the world differently. They look for ways to see things in their simplest form and, in most cases, this translates into appreciation for the design, philosophy, logic, or raw beauty.

Fourth epiphany leaders are endlessly amazed by people. They have a great appreciation for people who can do things that they cannot. When this happens, they become truly appreciative

172

and supportive. Fourth epiphany leaders find wonder in the capacity of people to endlessly surprise them with brilliance, ingenuity, and strength of will.

Appreciates What You Give And Reflects It Back To The Group

> "If I have seen further, it is by standing on the shoulders of giants."
>
> *Sir Isaac Newton*

When 4th epiphany leaders reflect on the accomplishments of their team, they naturally look for ways to show their appreciation. These leaders are in awe of those who contribute their excellent thoughts and abilities to help achieve the mission and reach the goal, and they understand that the greatest of motivators is appreciation. They are compelled to find ways to give back to the people that helped them achieve their mission and reach the vision.

Louis Kelso invented the first employee stock ownership plan. He did this so that the employees of a closely held newspaper could buy out their retiring owners. Until then, retiring owners would sell their assets and would place employees into an unknown future. Kelso believed that lawyers had a responsibility to improve society's institutions and support of democratic values. He saw the employee stock ownership plan as a way to democratize capital ownership. Now employees were able to participate in determining their own futures. Kelso changed the way business appreciated employees and introduced a new philosophy to the business world.

Google founders Larry Page and Sergey Brin have for years taken all of their Mountain View employees to a free skiing vacation at Squaw Valley, including transportation, food, lodging, entertainment, and of course lift tickets. Talk about setting a high standard for showing appreciation, Google is famous for giving back to its employees.

Herb Kelleher, co-founder and former CEO at Southwest Airlines, made the employees-first culture famous and made his airline profitable when others were struggling to just stay alive. Even when rival airlines were laying their employees off, Southwest Airlines never laid anyone off. The employees felt and appreciated the loyalty and responded by keeping Southwest Airlines profitable.

Suffer Not Fools

With 4th epiphany leaders, it may be hard to know where you stand in their minds sometimes, but there is an easy solution – just ask them. They will tell you. Most are very forthcoming in their evaluation of your abilities or worth to the organization and cause.

Famous for their swift action on employment decisions, a 4th epiphany leader may remove someone they don't see as helping their cause even if it isn't for nonperformance. Culture is of paramount importance to the 4th epiphany leader, and they are very sensitive to whether an employee's values and goals are effective for the organization. Remember that they are driven to succeed and anything or anyone that gets in their way will be overcome or removed.

On the flip side, many 4th epiphany leaders have experienced termination on these same grounds in their careers. Managers may find it difficult to direct and focus a 4th epiphany leader's energy. Fourth epiphany leaders are often misunderstood and their value is frequently underestimated, overlooked, or simply unrecognized as was the case for these 4th epiphany leaders: Steve Jobs was famously fired by the Apple board, Walt Disney was fired for lacking imagination, Albert Einstein was expelled from school, Thomas Edison was fired for not being productive enough, and Oprah Winfrey was fired for being unfit for TV.

Action Is King

> *"The most effective way to do it, is to do it."*
>
> *Amelia Earhart*

Action definitely speaks louder than words with 4th epiphany leaders. They are naturally an impatient bunch that has no qualms about calling people on their actions, regardless of how the individual explains themselves. These leaders always want to see results and want to get to the destination. It's as if they were kids in the backseat of a car constantly asking, "Are we there yet?"

They would be the first to say, "Don't tell me what you've done; show me." They want to understand and make sure activity actually helps their quest or mission. The 4th epiphany leader will be the one that walks into the lab and tries stuff. They understand the concept of sometimes asking forgiveness instead of permission. They appreciate leaders that take risks for the cause and think outside the norm. They value moving forward and that takes action and involves risk.

Looking at 4th epiphany behavior can be tricky because these leaders need to do whatever is necessary to help their people succeed. So I caution the reader again that these traits are even more difficult to nail down specifically because they are chameleons. If there is a defining trait for the 4th epiphany leader, I would have to say it's that they change things through their people whether it is their company, their industry, our perceptions, or the world.

The 4th Epiphany Leader's Meeting

As a thought exercise, let's imagine what a 4th epiphany leader might conduct the same meeting scenario we developed to understand how the other three levels of manager behaved. Keep in mind that this may not be the behavior you would see from a 4th epiphany leader. I offer this as an illustration to help give you insight as to what a difference the 4th epiphany makes.

Background & Setting: In an automotive parts manufacturing company employing over a thousand people, a mandatory meeting to discuss new safety requirements is scheduled. Notice of the meeting and a copy of the new safety requirements were sent out by management to the group of eight people a week before the meeting. The new safety requirements are to be implemented no later than four weeks from the meeting date. The meeting is to be held in a meeting room off the factory floor at the start of the shift, 8:00 a.m. The manager is the first-level supervisor.

Leader:	(Arriving about 1 minute early, the leader starts the meeting on time by reading, explaining, and asking everyone if they understand the new requirements.)
	What ideas do you have to meet the new requirement? What do we do about this?
George:	What if we require everyone to wear glasses?
Leader:	No, too restrictive. What's another way?
Maria:	Machine 14 is probably the only place that the new safety measure affects.

Leader: I would agree.

Chuck: What about barriers around the machine?

Leader: Probably still too restrictive, but let's go see.

(The group moves to the Machine 14 area.)

Tom: What if we do this?

(Draws transparent plastic machine guard on a pad of paper)

We can make it out of ballistic plastic.

Leader: Great idea, Tom.

(Asking the group) Opinions? Is this the best that we can do?

(Everyone nods or agrees verbally.)

Leader: Okay. Where do we get the plastic?

Gene: How about from Windshield Operations? They should have some over there.

Leader: Good. Go get it. I'll call the manager there and tell him you're coming. If I need to, I'll go over with you to make sure we can get some.

Now, for that design, I'm concerned about material flow.

Tom: No problem, the feed is from this side; we can mock it up this afternoon and have it ready for you to look at by 5:00 p.m.

Leader: If I came down at lunch and helped, could we have it done by the end of lunch and try it then? That way we would not affect production.

Tom: Okay. I'll bring the tools.

                 Gene, you get the plastic and we'll meet back here at noon.

Leader: Great. I'll bring sandwiches. Let's be the first to get this taken care of and on to reaching our goals. Thanks, everyone. See you at noon.

As you can see, the 4th epiphany leader pushes the group, moves obstacles, and appreciates the extra effort, while keeping the team on track to reach its production goals. With the 4th epiphany leader at the helm, everyone can be assured that if it can be done by the end of lunch, it will be done.

> *"A genuine leader is not a searcher for consensus but a molder of consensus. "*
>
> *Martin Luther King, Jr.*

Behaviors in 4th Epiphany-Led Organizations

As we turn now to concentrate on the reflective behaviors organizations exhibit in response to the actions of 4th epiphany leaders, we should recognize that their unique methods vary widely and, consequently, the reactions of organizations may encompass a large spectrum. The following are some of the reflective behaviors that I have seen most often when dealing or studying 4th-epiphany-led organizations and societies.

Outcomes Are What Matters

With a 4th-epiphany-led organization, everything will be geared toward results and moving forward to accomplish the mission or vision. Those who do the planning and support functions may not receive the credit that the line people do. If you are in a software development company, for example, programmers will be appreciated for what they do more than the facilities personnel who keep the lights on. Research and development will take center spotlight for achievements as opposed to the human resources department that hired the brilliant people. Those who produce the product get the credit; those who support the people who produce the product get some credit; and those who don't produce or discover are .... Well, let's just say they don't last long in a 4th-epiphany-led organization. No one cares how many reports you produce or if you have the right TPS coversheet. What they care about is how you answer the question: What have you done for us lately? What have you done to earn your right to be here?

Perception Is Important. I Reflect That.

Fourth-epiphany-led organizations normally have a well-developed sense of identity. They know and love their culture and are attuned to the fact that everything they do reflects on the organization's mission or cause. Everyone from the top leader to the newest member wants to be a part of these organizations because they are exciting places to be. Their messages or the perception of their causes are compelling and are usually viewed as honorable or at least benefiting society as a whole. Consequently, those who belong to these organizations are quite proud to belong to the group and wonder why everyone wouldn't want to be part of this very special organization.

These organizations typically have a logo, motto, or uniform of sorts that identifies its members. When I worked for Google, I actually thought the uniform was tennis shoes, shorts, backpack, and a tee-shirt with the Google logo on it. With Apple, it was much the same. Organizations such as Southwest Airlines actually had uniforms that most people wore, and wore proudly. Sometimes the uniform is a business suit, such as is common for bankers, stock brokers and attorneys.

People involved with 4th epiphany organizations are proud of their accomplishments and wish to be identified with them. They find ways to control that perception and make sure others know of their affiliation.

Tremendous Loyalty

Fourth epiphany leaders are some of the most loyal to their employees, and this loyalty is reflected back by the people in the organization. This is one of the rare traits that the organization directly reflects back to leadership. If a leader is loyal to their employees, the employees will be loyal to the leader. Notice that the loyalty is not for the organization; it is specifically for the leader.

It is often the case that, when a leader of this caliber leaves, many of their former employees eventually leave with them. This also goes for retirements as well. When a great leader retires from a company, there is ordinarily an uptick in retirements as well.

With 4th epiphany leaders, a group of insiders seems to develop around them that helps to run whatever organization they lead. These insiders can be anyone whom the leader trusts, and they are fiercely loyal as a result of that trust. Whether we are talking about an administrative assistant, the COO, or the chief of security, these individuals are personally connected to the 4th epiphany leader in ways that extend beyond the workplace. Fourth epiphany leaders tend to have few but very strong relationships in their personal life and work life.

More Than a Job

For most people there is a very large separation between work and home life; but this isn't the case with most people in 4th-epiphany-led organizations. In these tightly knit organizations, people seem to be able to blend their work and outside life homogeneously. They integrate their work into their entire lives and may seem to be working all the time. They may bring their dog to work, and their social network usually centers on people from work. It's not that they don't have a life. They just don't see their work as being work. It is stuff that they do that makes them happy – even if working for a 4th epiphany leader isn't all fun and games.

They may live up to exacting standards at work, but these people have a tendency to do the same at home. The main reason is that 4th epiphany organizations tend to draw these types of people to the group. Super achievers tend to draw other super achievers. For many, the distinction between life and work is blurred, but it matches their persona.

Their fuel is their belief that they are out to change the world in some form or fashion. They see their work in the organization not as a job, but as more of a calling. If you ask them, they typically have a difficult time defining their job and will usually default to listing their responsibilities.

Most people who work directly for 4th epiphany leaders are themselves driven to be the best, fastest, smartest, or other best of class. They have bought into the dream or vision of the leader with their hearts and minds, and they love their work. It's definitely more than a job to them; it's a way of life, a quest, a calling.

We Are Making a Difference

You can tell that this organization is made up of dedicated, focused people. They make a difference and know it. They can point to accomplishments that have changed the company, industry, or world. They thrive on this feeling. The 4th epiphany leader won't let them forget their accomplishments while driving for the next goal, the next world-changing event. They think differently and are proud of that. Given enough time and resources, they know they can accomplish anything.

We Believe

If you think you see a pattern here, you are correct. Most 4th-epiphany-led organizations don't just think they can make the vision a reality, they believe it. When you get people to believe in your vision, you have the total resources of their essence; and with that kind of commitment, you a can accomplish great things.

It's an affirmation and example of the self-fulfilling prophecy — they believe they can and so they do. In the 1960's, President Kennedy got us to believe that we could put a man on the moon by the end of the decade; and on July 21, 1969, Neil Armstrong stepped on the moon's surface and was later returned safely to Earth. An organization that believes is a force with which to be reckoned.

There Are No Boundaries

On a memorial to the U.S. Naval Construction Battalions (the Seabees) between Memorial Bridge and Arlington Cemetery:

> "The difficult we do immediately. The impossible takes a little longer."

If ever there were a motto of the organizations of 4th epiphany leaders, this would be it. Obviously, the Seabees have been led by 4th epiphany leaders. Imagine an entire organization that believes this. They will be the ones to go to new heights, change our perceptions, and make the rest of us think differently. They will be the ones to inspire us. Christopher Columbus understood that boundaries are only things that we put before ourselves.

> *"By prevailing over all obstacles and distractions, one may unfailingly arrive at his chosen goal or destination."*
>
> *Christopher Columbus*

If you tell a person in a 4th-epiphany-led organization that they can't do something, don't be surprised if they come back in a short time and show you that they can. People in 4th epiphany organizations have the leadership's permission and encouragement to try different things, to think outside the box – and actually, most of these people don't even know what the box is. If there is anyone that will draw the maps for the next generation to follow, it will be those that are in 4th-epiphany-led organizations.

We Are the Competition

When I worked for a large data center co-location provider, I was privy to the headquarters of several large Internet companies. During this time, these companies were in fierce competition for the Internet search market. When I visited Yahoo, there were signs up that said, "Beat Google!" When I traveled to Microsoft, again there were signs saying, "Beat Google!" A few months later, I started working at Google and I saw a sign on one of the cubicles that said, "Beat Google!"

Most 4th-epiphany-led organizations are so innovative that there is no one to beat but themselves. "Innovate or die" becomes their rallying call, and their tremendous capacity to focus on the possibilities they see as opposed to what others are doing normally helps them become leaders in their industry – but this can also be taken too far.

While it is normally quite healthy for leaders to encourage innovation wholeheartedly, if it is not kept in check, organizations can develop a not-invented-here mentality and miss the great things that are going on around them which could be used to help their own causes. Great organizations innovate by leapfrogging from great idea to great idea, regardless of where it came from. But when organizations and leaders cross this thin line of vanity, they can miss their own opportunities. Fourth epiphany leaders that remain clear about this danger are not above "stealing from the best" as some have put it, where "stealing" means learning and using the new discoveries of others as starting points of their own. It is part of what it means to stand on the shoulders of giants.

True 4th-epiphany-led organizations are not afraid to tear down what they just built in the quest to make it better. "If it's not broke, break it" can be heard in the hallways and boardroom. They see themselves as their toughest competition and they are most of the time correct.

An Organization of Leaders

If you look at a 4th-epiphany-led organization, you start to realize that it's filled with leaders and potential leaders. Fourth epiphany leaders are magnets for people who aspire to lead. They see the success of the leader and want to learn, emulate, and realize that success in their own lives. The environment 4th epiphany leaders create that supports the process of innovation is quite attractive to would-be leaders who wish to try their hands at the craft.

Because so many – in fact, almost everyone – in this organization likes to lead at something, they are given many opportunities to lead a project, small team, program, product, or an R&D effort. These organizations even go so far as to make leadership a topic of training and they try to identify would-be leaders. After all, fourth epiphany leaders want to help people be successful and that includes leadership too.

To be sure, 4th-epiphany-led organizations are unique to begin with; but if you find an organization that is touched at every level by 4th epiphany leaders, you are part of a very rare organization with the capability to do almost anything they set their sights on. Most 4th-epiphany-led organizations are small – less than 100 people. That's not to say that a 4th epiphany leader's influence can't reach all 100,000 people in a much larger organization or even a nation for that matter. But for the most part, I am limiting my discussion in this section to those who are directly managed or affected by the decisions of a 4th epiphany leader.

Working for a 4th Epiphany Leader

If you are lucky enough to run across a 4th epiphany leader and work for one, you will most probably find it to be a life-changing experience. Not that lightening strikes from the sky or anything, but 4th epiphany leaders have a way of getting you to see the world from a different perspective. Your first impression might be that this person is nuts. It's a common first impression; but as you later listen to their vision and sense their passion, you find yourself being drawn in. You want to know more; you become interested in the vision, the cause, or the mission of their organization. It seems to reach beyond just being profitable or improving the bottom line; the mission seems to be one that can make society better as a whole either through technology, innovation, or sheer determination.

On the flip side, they are relentless in their passion to achieve their vision and this translates to very challenging goals for employees. Fourth-epiphany leaders set perfection as their standard. And even though they wouldn't hold you to a standard they wouldn't measure themselves by, they do start with high standards and raise the bar from there. Naturally, the pressure to perform in these organizations can be extreme. They are demanding and can be very stressful organizations to work in, to say the least. So here are some ways to survive and thrive when working for a 4th epiphany leader.

Give Your Very Best

> *"Winning is not a sometime thing; it's an all time thing. You don't win once in a while, you don't do things right once in a while, you do them right all the time."*

> *Vince Lombardi*

The 4th epiphany leader only wants one thing, your very best – and they expect that you provide that every day that you come to work. My only advice is that you try to give it to them. Performance and exacting standards are just some of the high-stress attributes of this job; but if you can handle it, you will be successful.

If you work directly for the 4th epiphany leader, you can be sure that they will notice your efforts. They love to help those who give completely of themselves. Even if you are a level or two removed from the 4th epiphany leader, they will most probably still recognize your efforts. Fourth epiphany leaders like to catch people doing great things.

If you are not capable of giving 100 percent all the time, you may want to find another work situation. Fair warning: Fourth epiphany leaders demand and expect your very best.

Where Did That Come From?

Fourth epiphany leaders recognize that great ideas can come from anywhere and in most cases start off as some of the most outrageous suggestions. So what does this mean for you? Well, for one thing, it means that you shouldn't be afraid to make suggestions, no matter how strange or weird they seem.

Talk about an off-the-wall idea, remember Gary Dahl? Maybe not, but you have probably heard of his creation, the Pet Rock. The Pet Rock debuted in 1975 at $3.95 and, in just six months, Dahl sold more than 5 million of them. How about Doggles, eyewear for dogs? The business is doing just fine, thank you.

Unusual solutions to business problems sometimes come from a wish casually expressed as in this example from my personal experience. We were sitting around the meeting table thinking about the effort involved in supporting another group as they planned to swap out a production machine. The process being considered was to hire a rigging company to rig it out of the building. It would have required shutting production down for a couple of days, and the costs would have been enormous to rig it in and out. One of my employees said, "It sure would be easier if we could just drive the forklift in and carry it out." Everybody sighed, knowing that because of the raised floor it wasn't possible. But it actually got us to think, what if we just replaced the supports under the floor to carry the weight? We started doing calculations and, after some time, came up with some preliminary numbers that indicated that we could make the process pay off after only one machine move. The cost savings realized from the idea more than offset the expense of the modifications. What at first seemed like a silly idea actually made a great deal of sense once we took the time to evaluate it.

Don't be afraid to make suggestions with this leader no matter how strange or weird they seem to be.

Expand Your Thinking and Perception

"The measure of intelligence is the ability to change."

Albert Einstein

Chaos is the norm in the 4th epiphany leader's organization. It can be both physically and mentally challenging to say the least. Fourth epiphany leaders are truly open to new ideas and processes; they regularly try different things, even at the same time. Change will be the norm, so don't be surprised if the latest idea for production improvement comes from the leader reading an article that described the mating habits of ants.

Being in a 4th-epiphany-led organization will expose you to new ways to look at things, think about things, and even how to think about things. This is your chance to broaden your horizons, learn with abandon, and try new stuff.

One other thing I suggest you do is volunteer. Volunteer even for things that you have no idea what they are. This does several things for you: First, it gives you exposure to new people, new settings, new processes, and new thinking; and, second, it signals your willingness to try new things which will put you high on the leader's list of go-to people when new and exciting things come up. Enjoy the ride.

Be Conscious When Speaking, But Take the Reins

Fourth epiphany leaders are always looking for other potential leaders to continue their legacy. The 4th epiphany leaders I have known personally have all had a sixth sense when it comes to identifying future leaders. And to that end, I recommend that you always do your homework or research because whenever you have the occasion to interact with them -- even if it is on a subject you would reasonably believe they would have little knowledge of – it is not uncommon for them to become a quasi-expert overnight about your topic. I once spoke off the cuff about quantum physics and the next day this 4th epiphany leader had me chatting with a Nobel Laureate (his personal friend) on the subject. I survived the conversations and learned a great deal; but I came away with a new epiphany – most 4th epiphany leaders have very interesting friends. Be careful what you say!

One way to impress this leader is to develop processes that automate, eliminate, or make things easier. They are all about innovation and being proactive. They appreciate it. Fourth epiphany leaders are not afraid of intelligence or innovation; they welcome it and seek it out. Other managers may be scared of being outdone or not being seen as the leader; but the 4th epiphany leader loves to see their people succeed. So go ahead and develop that project that you have been thinking about. The only caution is that you make sure to accomplish what has been asked of you.

Don't be afraid to take the reins of a project and show this leader what you can accomplish given the resources at hand. Take every opportunity to lead. A 4th epiphany leader will help mentor you or make sure that someone will help you. Great leaders appreciate people who strive to become better and to make the world they live in a better place.

Take Responsibility

This small sign sat on President Harry Truman's desk: "The buck stops here." But 4th epiphany leaders don't actually care who is to blame when things don't go as expected. Their interest is to see that the organization learns not to make the same mistakes again. If you see that something you have done did not work out as expected, accept the responsibility and move on. A 4th epiphany leader will see that as a sign of moral strength which will earn their trust, as long as you do learn the lesson.

Try, accept responsibility, learn, and try again – 4th epiphany leaders understand this cycle as they are continually doing the same thing.

The Emperor Is Not Wearing Any Clothes

Don't be afraid to disagree or ask for clarification. Fourth epiphany leaders sometimes need to re-evaluate their direction and appreciate different perspectives from others. During meetings ask them to help you understand the thinking or logic for their decision or direction. You wouldn't want to make a habit of it, but occasionally this is fine.

These leaders value the different perspectives and experiences that each person brings to the table, and they recognize that those differences can lead them to some very interesting insights into what they are trying to accomplish. Because they trust that you will help the organization keep moving in the direction of the vision and goals, your comments and suggestions will be taken as valuable input toward their objectives.

Develop Your Own Measures of Success

Define goals for yourself and keep others in the organization – and particularly the 4th epiphany leader – aware of your progress. This will help you in a number of ways. First, this is a great way to share how well you are doing; and if you need help in a specific area, it gives the leader the opportunity to assist you. It's a great way to develop a good reputation for transparency as it showcases your thoughts and ability.

When you develop ways to measure your own success, you set expectations for yourself that others will recognize as an ability to self-direct. The measures need to be specific to your needs and should be so granular that you can monitor and update them daily. They also need to be visible so that they have top-of-mind awareness. Your 4th epiphany leader, and other people in the organization, will also appreciate knowing what you spend your time doing.

By setting your own goals and measures of success, you invite participation into your direction, help determine how your effort should be evaluated, and set a great example for others in the organization. It's a great way to show the world your talent and abilities. Let your light shine!

Take One Step up Every Day

Review your goals: Are they supportive of the organization's mission and vision? Do they support what the leader wants to do? Your personal goals for work need to help the organization and the leader reach the vision that has been articulated for you. Is your goal to make the world's best widgets? Then you should be able to define how what you are doing helps the organization do that.

Ask yourself what a 4th epiphany leader would ask you: "What have you done for us today?" Can you show daily progress on your goals? By prominently displaying your goals and progress, you subconsciously remind yourself and others that you are not going to reach the summit of this mountain in one superhuman-like leap, but, rather, by taking at least one step up every day.

If you are a leader in the organization, you are responsible for making it possible for your people to take that one step up every day. What did you do today to make that happen? As a leader, your role is not to instill an attitude of achieving goals from your desk. You must take an active part in seeing that goals are reached every day. After all, it is we that must lead the way up the mountain. But when progress is not being made as expected or desired, you should mirror the approach a 4th epiphany leader would take in this situation. A 4th epiphany leader will not chastise those that are responsible for poor progress; they will help them succeed – and that should be your example. Have you taken a step up today?

Take Time Off To Sharpen the Saw

Working in a 4th-epiphany-led organization is stressful and many times relentless. Take time off. There is a story of woodcutters that has been told many times in many ways that provides a metaphor for taking time off. Here is my rendition:

Two wood cutters were talking one day and they argued over who was the fastest wood cutter in the area. Each thought that they were the best. To finally put an end to the discussion, they proposed a competition. Whoever cut the most wood in one day would be the winner and have bragging rights.

At sunrise the next day, both started cutting wood. As the first woodcutter worked continuously throughout the morning, he heard the second woodcutter stop and rest. He thought to himself, if I don't rest, I'll cut more wood than he will and I'll be known as the best. So the first woodcutter worked constantly through lunch and non-stop into the afternoon to the agreed time to stop.

A town official was asked to measure the wood that was cut by both. Upon measuring, the official declared the second woodcutter the winner. The first woodcutter was astonished. "How could he have beaten me?"

He confronted the second woodcutter and asked him, "How did you beat me? I worked continuously. I heard you stop and rest."

The second woodcutter said, "I never rested; I only stopped to sharpen my saw."

Sharpen-the-saw stories are metaphors for renewal; renewal of our spirits, our minds, and our bodies. Even machines need to have some downtime for renewal or they will fail. Humans are the same. You must take time off.

The 4th epiphany leader knows that time off is important and will more than likely demand that you take time off anyway. Don't be surprised if they even demand that you leave your phone at work when you go on vacation.

Do You Love What You Do?

Do you love what you do or tolerate what you do? Are you hoping for something better or do you feel that you are home when you come to work? In a 4th epiphany organization, most likely you will either love it or hate it. There doesn't seem to be an in-between with these organizations or leaders.

The answer to this question should be considered sincerely and with great care. If you find that you do love it, then you are probably in the right place. If you find that you tolerate it but like some of the attributes, then it may be better to move on in the long run. People who don't buy into the vision of the 4th epiphany leader will eventually grow tired of the constant pursuit of the vision. It is not difficult for the 4th epiphany leader to be aware of whether a person is all-in for the organization and the mission they are about.

Are you where you want to be? Does the vision of the future energize you? Do you love what you do?

What Do You Want To Be When You Grow Up?

During an interview with a 4th epiphany leader, don't be surprised if you are asked, "What do you want to be when you grow up?" They want to know what your plans are for the future. What they are really asking is, Are those future plans compatible with what the organization needs? Fourth epiphany leaders are interested in the whole person, not just the one that shows up between 9:00 to 5:00.

When working for a 4th-epiphany-led organization, where does your life plan fall in helping the organization reach its future vision? Can you see yourself working for the organization in five years, ten years – how about forty? It is not uncommon for a 4th epiphany leader to think about how you would fit into the organization or what you could bring to the organization over an extended period of time.

Be Prepared For the Deep End of the Pool – Or Not

One of the behaviors I see constantly from 4th epiphany leaders is that they commonly throw people into the deep end of the pool – essentially, they commonly give people responsibilities that are much greater than they have dealt with in the past to see how they do. They expect the best from everyone, and this is how they get it. Many of these leaders seem to know other people's limits better than they do.

Most people can handle this a few times, but 4th epiphany leaders do this most all the time. They constantly want to get the most out of each person, and they enjoy watching them grow. Count on being tested, stressed, and given more responsibility than you ever had in the past.

You can relish the opportunity to show the leader what you can do, or fear it. If you find yourself fearing it, again, it might be a sign that you should seek a different situation. If you look forward to the challenges, then you need to prepare yourself. I'm not sure what specifics you would need to prepare for, but you should be asking others about their experiences and how they succeeded. What advice would they offer? What general skills do you need, and where can you learn them?

One consolation: The 4th epiphany leader will normally not throw you into water so deep that you cannot bounce off the bottom. In other words, they will strive to help you grow and learn but not try to drown you. After all, they want you to succeed and they have a genuine and vested interest in your success.

Many people don't talk about working for 4th epiphany leaders except in terms of surviving it. For most people, working for this level or type of leader may not be a pleasant experience. The 4th epiphany leader expects the best from everyone, is relentless in the pursuit of their vision, and loves change. It is exciting and can be very profitable in many respects – financially, professionally, and personally. If you do get the opportunity to work for one, count yourself lucky as there are not many of them out there and you will at the very least have an exciting experience.

Pathways to the Next Epiphanies

While I truly believe that this 4th epiphany is what will take you from being a manager to being a leader, the journey of becoming a great leader never really ends. There is so much to learn about people and what inspires them that you can literally spend a lifetime mastering the profession. This section is dedicated to those who have made a commitment to leadership and recognize that there is more to discover. Through the following discussions and recommended actions, I start to lay out the tools, techniques, and understanding that can help you explore the many facets of leadership and organizational dynamics. However, you must recognize that the needs of each group are different and you will need to determine what is suitable for you to know in order to achieve your vision for the future.

Performance Curve

Every group has a performance curve. Some are steep; some are not. Some peak quickly and degrade rapidly; others peak very slowly and stay at high levels of performance over long periods of time. The shape of that performance curve is actually a function of the leadership, the ability of the group to learn and innovate, and the amount of passion or motivation for the vision.

A group's success can be predicted by several factors. Of these is something called Group Vision Acquisition Persistence (GVAP), and it is basically a measure of the group's passion and perseverance in the obtainment of its vision for the future. Some of the factors that go into this are directly attributable to the leader, such as:

Vision Attachment – This has to do with how the vision or mission of the group is perceived by each person. Do they understand what it is? Do they personally identify with it? Do they see themselves as able to help achieve it? Through precise, targeted articulation of the vision, the leader can achieve each of these for a wide population of the group if they know their audience and can put the vision in the vernacular associated with the group perception of the situation.

Vision Saturation – Simply stated, this is the percentage of the group's population that knows, understands, and accepts the vision or mission.

Group Vision Focus – This is how much time the group's activities directly support the obtainment of the vision or mission. The leader can increase the group's focus on vision obtainment by manipulating policy, organizational design, and engaging in focused monitoring.

Not all performance curves are good for all organizations. A very steep curve to success has its problems and issues as does one that slowly ramps up at a snail's pace. Most organizations wish to have longevity in decades or centuries and, for the most part, the success curves for these sustained successful organizations will have slow ramp-ups (usually in years), with slowly increasing slopes over very long periods of time. This is desirable for many companies, but not as good for volunteer groups or airlines.

The interesting thing about performance curves of groups is that every organization that I have found also had a period of degradation, usually associated with the death or exit of the leader. Sustained high performance over decades and centuries is very difficult. The only examples I have found that could achieve this longevity have either national (regional) or religious affiliations. As they say, nothing lasts forever, and I suspect it is the case with group performance as well.

So given this limitation of organizational performance, the best a leader can do is to use the traits and organizational factors available to them while they are active in the organization to get the group to reach high performance and sustain it for as long a period as possible.

Tremendous Energy Output All the Time

The implication of these performance curves outlined above is that I believe that all groups will eventually see their performance degrade to some lower level which may even cause the disintegration of the group. The reason for this is that the tremendous energy output of the group in the quest to obtain its vision or mission typically does not last. People have a tremendous capacity for extraordinary effort over very long periods; but eventually they burn out, move on, or lose interest.

There are two ways a leader can combat this inevitable outcome: They can continually bring in new people with the energy to recharge the group or they can find ways to re-energize the members of the group. The success of either will depend on the vision/mission and what it takes to get vision attachment and saturation for new people, and what can cause a re-attachment and focus for those already in the organization. Either method requires energy to counter the effects of performance degradation.

A special issue with those already in the organization is burnout – the condition of a person that is mentally and physically tired from the pursuit of the goals. They need time off to sharpen the saw. The only solution to this is something akin to a sabbatical, the length and particulars of which depend on the individual's specific needs and situation.

It goes without saying that the leader is responsible for the health and well-being of their organization. Learn about groups and people in general, and find out what you can do to help them succeed.

Student of Human Behavior – A Lifetime of Learning

Leadership at this level is a lifetime career choice. We elect to be leaders, in spite of all that it entails. Our specialty is the leadership of people, and so we must become students of human behavior. We must study the behavior of people in groups and by themselves, when stressed and when inspired. The spectrum of human behavior is endlessly expanding and changing. Just 100 years ago, leaders were concerned only about meeting legal requirements. They literally told people where to go and what to do. Today we must entice the best people with visions that inspire them to help us change the world, or just change our companies.

New information and knowledge is added to the study of human behavior all the time now. And because of the never-ending complexity, the leader must constantly learn to help inspire and lead. I doubt that we will ever learn all there is to know about how to inspire and motivate people to action, and so, in and of itself, it becomes another lifelong endeavor and subject of study.

Take classes, read the latest articles and books, go to seminars, and go to discussion groups about leadership. Learn new techniques about why people do what they do and how to find great people to help reach the vision. Never stop learning.

Try Stuff – Different Stuff

If you are not trying something different every day, you are falling behind. Whether or not you believe that the new process or thing will work, if someone in your organization believes in it, try it. I'm not saying bet the farm, but I encourage you to try things that other people are passionate about. This helps cement the trust relationship between you and those who want the opportunity to put their ideas into play. But it might also lead to something that works better. As I mentioned before, think of the Babe Ruth school of success and go to bat as many times as you can. Hitting home runs is a numbers game; and the more times you go to bat, the better your chances are that you will hit that home run.

You should push your managers to do the same. Increase your chances at finding the next diamond in the rough, the next billion dollar business line, or the next Nobel Prize-winning idea. You will never know unless you try.

Develop and support the culture of trying stuff in your organization. Find ways to support the culture, and find ways to support the managers and leaders that support that culture. They are your future; they are the people that will drive innovation in the organization. Make it a cultural norm, the standard by which everyone lives. Your future and the future of your organization actually depend on it. It is the only way that you can keep the organization performing at a high level.

Take One Step Every Day

In association with trying stuff, your organization also needs to continually move forward. Otherwise, they will be left behind. All markets, industries, and organizational environments change. They do so because of outside pressures to perform better, faster, or more efficiently, or because new technologies permit innovation. Your organization must constantly innovate and improve in order to stay relevant. It is like climbing a mountain. You won't leap to the summit every day, but you must take at least one step toward the vision every day.

What are you going to do today to lead your organization to take those steps? What have your people tried today that was different? Whatever means you use, the steps must be measurable by the people or person having to change. You have to make the steps an expectation of yourself and of others, so make them visible. Put them on your calendar, in your personal goals, and publicize them. There is nothing like peer pressure to help you make taking steps an everyday habit.

Focus On Your Strengths

I have often heard that you should identify your weaknesses and work to make them strengths. I am not a fan of this philosophy. Your strengths are your strengths for a reason. You focused on them; you worked to make them your strengths; so why would you abandon them now? My recommendation is to continue to make them even stronger. Focus on them, spend time doing them and become even better. If Mark Spitz had followed this philosophy, he might have focused on basketball (let's just assume it is one of his weaknesses.) Instead, he focused on his strength, swimming, and won seven gold medals, simultaneously setting seven new world records in the 1972 Olympics.

My recommendation is that you focus on your strengths and hire to cover for your weaknesses. Out there somewhere is someone that has great strengths in your areas of weakness. If you think about it, two people who complement each other in this manner are stronger than either one could hope to be. If you follow the work-on-your-weaknesses philosophy, you would have two people that are struggling. It makes better sense to have two people who are focusing and working within their strengths.

You can also apply this to your organization. Focus on its strengths. I have seen many times companies that lose their focus – in other words, they do things that are not their strengths – and fail because of it. Hire to fill the weakness holes if you need to.

10,000 Hours

In his book *"Outliers"*, Malcolm Gladwell talks about how 10,000 hours of practice or experience is one of the things that determine success. Simply stated, the premise is that if you spend enough time doing whatever it is, you can learn it and, through practice, become really good at it. This makes sense on its face – spend time doing something and get better. So how can you apply this to leadership?

When you think about it, as a person in a leadership position, you can get 10,000 hours of experience in about five years (approximately 2,000 hours/year) but in reality, not all of this time is spent in leadership activities. There is a great deal of time spent reviewing reports, timesheets, projects, and other activities that are really not leadership experience. If I estimate the actual time that I spent in true leadership activities, I would have to say it would be closer to 30 percent of my time when I was a less experienced manager and up to 70 percent as I became a senior leader. So if 50 percent is actual leadership experience, it pushes the time frame out to about ten years to get that 10,000 hours of experience.

While I believe that ten years of experience is good, I still believe in Vince Lombardi's words, "Perfect practice makes perfect." I'm sure that not everything I did would have been considered "perfect" by Coach Lombardi. So if I add in the learning curve for leadership, I'm thinking that becoming an experienced, great leader would take the better part of twenty years. So if you are eighteen when you start in leadership opportunities, then by age thirty-eight or so you should be a great leader or at least have the skills, knowledge, and experience to become one.

While this maybe a pretty good thought exercise, the exact time of when you become a great leader actually depends more on your epiphanies and how they change your values and behaviors. To give you an example, Joan of Arc was only seventeen when she led the French Army into battle and victory. She turned a dismal situation into one of hope by tying it to a spiritual inspiration. Some would call her leadership the turning point in the Hundred Years War.

You can realize what it takes to inspire, motivate, and lead people at any age; but to do it well, that requires practice. Some people are capable of working within the natural landscape of human behavior with ease. They are labeled "natural leaders" or "born leaders." But even with this innate understanding of human behavior, the leader must be grounded in widely held values and have a very compelling vision in order to be successful.

As for my recommendations, practice leadership whenever you can. If you are not in a position of leadership, volunteer for one. Lead Cub Scouts, a church function, or anything else where you can practice being a leader. None of us are perfect, but with perfect practice, we can become very good at it.

Catch People Doing Great Things

> *"Never interrupt someone doing something you said couldn't be done."*

> *Amelia Earhart*

Hewlett Packard had a system of management that was dubbed Management By Walking Around (MBWA). It was designed to get managers out from behind their desks and into the areas that they were responsible for. It was great for catching things that weren't quite going right, and management could then make the associated changes to correct or mitigate the situation. This practice had a couple of different effects on the labor force – one negative and one positive depending on management behavior.

If you knew that every time your manager came into your area that they would find something wrong and make a report of it, how would you start to feel or behave? How do you think that a workforce would react to this?

Imagine if every time your manager came to your area they found something good. Now, imagine if they recognized your effort. I'm guessing that you would look forward to the manager coming to your area so that you could show off your latest idea and how it's working. Imagine how this would affect the workforce.

Catch people doing amazing things out there. They do it every day. If you are really lucky, you will catch them doing what was once thought of as impossible.

Find Reasons to Celebrate Every Day

There have been many studies that show that we like to be around people who have positive outlooks on life. We enjoy being around those that seem to enjoy the simple things and who always seem have a smile for us. We have a tendency to listen to them and find it easier to learn from them.

Find reasons to celebrate every day. Whether it is for a beautiful, sunny day, the rain that we needed, the new process that is working better than expected, or a great parking spot, tell people about it. This shows people that you appreciate it when good things happen, that you care and you pay attention.

While we all have bad hair days, the leader is still under the organizational microscope and, if you have a bad day, this action will grant permission for others to have bad days too. Be the example and point out to others reasons to celebrate. Find reasons to help others and to be thankful for the things that we do have. I'm not saying that you have to be religious about this, just that people are affected by what you do and they have a tendency to follow and be inspired by those who seem to love life.

Try this for a week and see what happens: Tell just one person a day about something that you appreciate, admire, or are thankful for. You just might have something to celebrate after you do this. What could it hurt?

Never Assign Things That You Wouldn't Do Yourself

Never assign anyone a task that you wouldn't be willing to do yourself. Perhaps an experience I had in the Navy would illustrate what I mean.

I was initially stationed to a submarine that was in overhaul, basically being rebuilt in a shipyard. We were getting to the end of the overhaul and it was necessary to clean the ship to put it back to fighting condition. For those of you that are familiar with construction sites, you know that dirt and debris are everywhere. The same is true for a submarine during overhaul.

We had a big cleaning job to do. My assignment was to clean the bilges in an area under the diesel generator, one of the worst areas. I had to put on coveralls, climb under the diesel into the bilges, and clean out all the debris and dirt. It was a miserable job, to say the least. I had a helper who climbed under the diesel with me to help out. We spent a good two hours working under the diesel and found ourselves even joking about the stuff we might find and whether it would be alive or ...?

When the job was done, my new friend (Bob) and I were covered from head to toe in grease, grime, and who knows what, but the area under the diesel was clean. As we stood next to the diesel and began to strip off our coveralls, I asked Bob what he did on the ship. It was only then that I saw the two silver oak leaves on his collars as he started to remove his coveralls. He said he was the captain. I was too shocked to say anything. Here the captain of the ship had spent the last two hours helping me clean out one of the dirtiest places on the ship. He said, "You look surprised." I had trouble forming sentences in that moment.

He just smiled and told me that as a leader he needed to show everyone that on a submarine there is no job that is beneath anyone on the ship, that every job is important because our lives depend on the job being done right – even my assignment to clean out the bilges. It's true. The bilges pump out the water when the ship has a leak. If the bilges are full of debris, it will clog the strainers and the bilge pumps won't work. When you consider how critical a flooding incident is on a submarine, you realize that the captain was correct to have this perspective.

Commander Robert Mitchell's lessons on leadership had a profound effect on me and stick with me to this day. His simple act did more than just alleviate his need to make sure the job was done correctly. It inspired his crew and officers to think differently about their jobs and the importance of leading by example. I believe to this day that Commander Mitchell would have performed any task that he asked his crew to do.

Leaders are teachers by default of their position. And since people learn by hearing, seeing, and practicing, it is our job as leaders to tell, show, and uphold expectations for the behaviors we want to exist in our organization.

Publish

In the world of academia, the unwritten rule is "Publish or perish." In academia, if you're not moving forward and telling the world of your discoveries, you're rapidly becoming obsolete – and so is your career. As a leader, you should publish the lessons that you have learned in your career and share them with the next generation of leaders.

Publishing or being published on a subject will normally make you the expert or go-to person for that topic, but it can benefit your career in leadership in other ways as well. It is, first and foremost, an effective way to make your values and philosophies known. But it also tells the people in your organization, both above and below, that they have an expert in their midst to whom they can refer.

Another benefit is that writing helps you articulate your ideas and thoughts. It makes you consider and clarify the specific phrases, structure, and words that will bring the reader to the same thoughts that you have while writing. With leadership, the more clearly you can articulate a vision, idea, or thought in another person, the more likely that you will be able to inspire them.

Publish: Volunteer to write a blog piece, a white paper, or monthly article in the company or organization's periodical.

Go back to school and take a writing class or other class that helps you organize your thoughts and present them in writing.

Keep a Published Perspective

> *"Everyone's an example – some of what to do and some of what not to do."*

> *Paul M. Vergon (my father)*

I was once asked if I wanted my emails to show up on the front page of the *"Wall Street Journal."* Not that there is a good chance of that, but it did make me think about what I said and how I said it. In today's world, many of the things that leaders say, write, and do can and do wind up on the front page.

So when you write that email or that memo, consider the ramifications of its being made public. What do you want to show the world? What side of you do you want people to see? We all have immediate reactions to situations. Not all of them are good for leaders to exhibit. Take two seconds to consider your actions and words before they become public (by "public" I mean leaving your mouth or hand to go into the world). This also goes back to being the example.

Take two seconds and consider: Is this the example that you want to share?

Quick Caveat: Emails last forever and private texts may not be private. It will serve you well if you live by the old adage that whatever you say and do will wind up on the front page of the *"Wall Street Journal."* In many ways, the world of Mr. Orwell's *"1984"* has come true for leaders. We live under the microscope.

Explore Ethics and Values as Thought Exercises

In our careers as leaders, we will be confronted with questions of ethics and values. What if you couldn't get a building permit in a foreign country without offering the local officials an offering of good faith? What if a prospective large client indicated they would only consider your proposal while they were at a local strip club? What would you do if you found out that one of your high-level, critical-function managers was secretly having an affair with his administrative assistant?

You should at least consider some of the situations that could arise and that you may encounter. Spend a little time considering your options, course of action, and responses to such situations. Where are you going to stand? What values are you unwilling to change? What do you expect of your people when they are confronted with similar situations? What situations would stir you to action, to speak up for others, and to defend the high road?

Give thought to these possible situations because, at some time, you will have to face them.

Learn From Other 4th Epiphany Leaders

If you want to learn about leadership, follow the leaders. Join groups that have other 4th epiphany leaders in them. Learn from them, share with them, and support them. Like anyone, we all need a little support.

If you are lucky enough to be mentored by one, have them suggest clubs, organizations, or groups from which you can benefit. Many times you will find that someone out there has been or is facing similar situations and may have a great way of handling it or a solution that you haven't considered.

I would not recommend online social networks, however. I feel a certain trepidation not knowing the individual with whom I am sharing my thoughts. You could discover that you are actually conversing with your boss, people who work for you, or a member of the press. If you need to maintain an online presence, however, it is best to carefully consider everything you share. You may find it best to consult a social media expert to help guide your efforts in this direction.

Service clubs, schools and universities, and conferences are all great places to meet other leaders. Schools and universities are often frequented by leaders because they never stop learning. It's fairly easy to spot leaders at industry conferences since they are often surrounded by the attendees, but be careful not to overlook those that are quietly changing the world in the corners.

Get out there and network! What you learn could make all the difference.

Teach

> *"If you think in terms of a year, plant a seed; if in terms of ten years, plant trees; if in terms of 100 years, teach the people."*

> *Confucius*

Joseph Joubert said, "To teach is to learn twice." The benefits from teaching can be many. While you must learn the material well enough to teach it, you must also learn how to convey that knowledge to your audience. This conveying of knowledge is a vital skill for any leader. Practice it. Teaching people garners their respect, increases your value to the organization, and continually allows you to practice inspiring them. You learn to shape thoughts and ideas, to plant the seeds of inquiry and questions of what could be.

Take classes to learn how people learn, what works effectively, and how to engage people's minds. Learn how to determine if what you are teaching is being retained *and* is changing behaviors. In many cases, what you teach people will be your legacy.

Have Courage to Do What Is Right

> *"Courage is what it takes to stand up and speak; courage is also what it takes to sit down and listen."*
>
> *Winston Churchill*

As a leader in your organization, you will need courage to accomplish the things that will truly make a difference. You need to trust your instincts and sometimes go against even your past experiences to move to a new level of leadership. Let's look at some of the situations that can test a person's character and courage.

- *Accepting responsibility for the actions of your group*

Accepting the responsibility for the actions of your group when things don't go as planned is always a test for leaders. We empower others to act on our behalf and we need to accept responsibility for that. One of the things that my father taught me early was that, if it happens in my group, it's my responsibility. I was the one who set the expectations, goals, and approved the processes. The only exception is when a person is clearly acting in a criminal manner, that is, if you specifically stated that the action was not sanctioned through direct orders or policies.

It takes courage to admit that your leadership led to an unsatisfactory result, but it would reflect on your lack of leadership if you don't. The situation should be a learning experience for all. Just make sure that you and others learn from the situation and don't repeat it. Admit it, learn from it, change what needs to be changed, and move on.

> *"Even if you fall on your face, you're still moving forward."*
>
> *Victor Kiam*

- *Standing on your morals or values*

There may come a time when you have to make a decision between your morals or personal values and your job. This situation doesn't happen to most people very often; but since leaders deal with wide variety of issues, they are more likely to encounter this type of difficulty.

What morals or values are you unwilling to change? Are you willing to place your fiscal health at risk for this? It takes courage to stand up for what you believe and even more to act upon your convictions. I have actually quit a job due to my feelings around what I was being asked to do. You may have to make that decision yourself someday.

- *Making a report to authorities*

When you have exhausted all other avenues of attempting to address the situation internally or the situation is of such grave nature that it warrants notification to the proper authorities, will you do it? You might wonder, will whistleblower laws protect me? What would happen to my career if I didn't report this? Can I be found complicit for not reporting this?

Do you have the courage to do what is right? We have seen many times in the news where people in positions of responsibility chose to ignore very serious or even heinous situations to protect their careers or their reputations. It takes courage to report these situations and to make sure that they are properly addressed.

- *To sacrifice the cash cow and commit to new markets*

Can you imagine the discussions that took place when Steve Jobs wanted to enter the cell phone market? After all, Apple was a computer company, wasn't it? Or what about when then-president Andy Grove and CEO Gordon Moore at Intel in 1985 decided to drop its longtime cash cow (memory chips) and move into the processor market?

We look at these moves now and think how brilliant they were, but at the time they seemed crazy by most outsiders – and insiders as well. It takes courage to follow your heart or gut and take the organization into new territory. President Lincoln did it with the Emancipation Proclamation. Are you going to be brave enough when the time comes for you to ignore the naysayers and lead the organization into some new direction? To be a true leader sometimes requires bucking trends and, in homage to *"Star Trek,"* to go where no person has gone before.

- *To hire the best person for the job*

Sometimes the best person for the job is not the one that fits the best with the organization. There can be a lot of advantages to diversifying your workforce and adding different perspectives, especially on the leadership team. Instead of skills and experience, why not look for perspective, values, and passion? What would happen if you changed the hiring criteria to the latter?

What would you have to do to convince your Human Resources (HR) department that the job descriptions need to be scrapped and rewritten with passion as a critical job trait? But imagine the things that your organization could do if you were to do just that. It makes you wonder why we don't list passion on the job description.

- *To allow another to lead*

As the quote from Winston Churchill stated, "… courage is also what it takes to sit down and listen." Sometimes it is the right thing to be quiet and let someone else lead. This can be scary, especially when you have so much invested physically and mentally. Allowing others to lead helps develop them and can give you a sense of their readiness for leadership.

It takes courage to allow others to lead; but the rewards can be great, especially if you find someone that can carry the load while you're away. You do want to take vacations, don't you?

- *To lead people to new heights*

As a 4th epiphany leader, you understand people. You have a good grasp of what you are about and have a vision for the organization. You must also have the courage to take the first steps and keep going even in the face of opposition. Just remember what Henry Ford said: "Obstacles are those frightful things you see when you take your eyes off the goal." Stays focused and do what needs to be done. Lead, inspire, and take the organization to new heights.

I can't imagine the situations you will face as a leader, but I do know that, for some, you will need courage to face them. You will need courage to overcome and prevail.

"Courage is the price that life exacts for granting peace."

Amelia Earhart

─────────────────────────────

These are some of the things that you can do as a 4th epiphany leader for personal growth and constant improvement. As you know, your calling is to help people be successful, and that includes you too. If you have made it this far, you have the basic foundation to be a great leader. Your own personal situation will dictate what other epiphanies you will need to experience in order for you to move to great heights. Being a great leader is about constantly learning your craft, inspiring people to become more than they ever thought they could be and, in doing so, improving the human condition.

The 4th Epiphany

Chapter 6

Understanding Influence, a Vital Epiphany

Every leader must understand the vital difference between influence and control. Otherwise, they will not become effective or great leaders. They can experience this epiphany at any time in their journey and, therefore, it is not listed in order with the others. But nonetheless, it is absolutely vital to the development of every successful leader.

By control, I mean that you can positively determine the outcome. So if you think about control from that perspective, what is it that you can actually control? Other people are not under your control unless you physically restrain them or physically move them. I know that some will take issue with this, but it is the reality of our world. Even if you put a gun to someone's head and order them to do something, they can still elect not to do it. They have a choice. In this situation, you may have a very strong influence over the individual, but you do not have control. In reality, control is an illusion at best.

A Vital Epiphany

Influence is all that we really have as leaders

As leaders, how do we create influence? How do we increase our influence? What kinds of influence can we have? Influence over people can take two very basic forms – influence by threat of something undesirable or the possibility of something desirable. In today's world, we are bombarded all the time by both types of influence. Television advertising is a good example. Half the time we are offered a product that makes us look better, feel better, or increases our status in society; the other half of the time we are told that if we don't buy the product we will continue to suffer, not look as good, and not be as acceptable in society. Political ads constantly tell us how selecting one candidate over another will improve our lives or make us worse off.

Leaders use influence to make things happen: They compel people to action and attract people to their causes and organizations. The most common means of influencing people is by articulating a desirable future state. Simply put, they inspire us. Managers, on the other hand, use both the threat of being fired and the possibility of a bonus if we meet some high expectation. Each of these methods of influencing people has different effects and outcomes when used.

Influence: Tools of the Leader and Manager

As we delve into the subject of influence, let's consider when positive and negative influences are used and what the most probable outcomes are. But keep in mind that it is difficult to predict potential outcomes with any degree of accuracy, particularly if you're trying to be specific as to individuals. The most probable outcomes will be more applicable to larger groups. I will try to give a most probable outcome for each type of influence. And though this does not comprise the complete list of influencers, they are what I see most commonly.

Negative Influence Tools

Direct Threats

A direct threat is some type of undesirable action that is directed at you by a person. Examples are a gun in your face, a spanking if you don't clean up your room or a statement such as

"I'll fire you if that isn't done by 4:00 p.m." Most direct threats are fairly effective in gaining action toward the desired state, but do very little to cause desired behaviors. Direct threats are very detrimental and do nothing to develop effective organizations. If a threat exceeds someone's personal value level for retribution or revenge, outcomes can become very serious. You can get everything from malicious compliance to someone responding with lethal force. At best, they will leave as soon as possible.

Fear of Outcomes

We see fear of outcomes used all the time in advertising and political ads. Most examples take the form "Do this or this will happen" with the outcome being a less desirable outcome for the person, group, or organization. Most of the time, fear of outcomes is used to motivate people to make a choice. "Vote for Smith, because Jones will raise your taxes." Your doctor would use this to tell you to lose weight or become diabetic. Parents use this with children: "Don't touch that or you will burn your hand" or "Do your homework or you will get bad grades."

For this to work, the people being influenced must have the perception that the potential outcomes are actually true. If this is not the case, the method will not work at all. The key indicator for effective compliance is acceptance of the underlying premise.

Fear of outcomes has been used effectively by many leaders. Gandhi used it in messages to the people and England – Effect change or we will continue to be defiant. Reagan used it to make us fear the communistic form of government and the overreach of regulations. Hitler used it to make the general population blame Jews for their plight and to motivate his people toward the "final solution." Fear of outcomes can be a very effective influence, if the premise is believed. However, the repercussions are that you must always make someone or something the undesirable. On the other hand, when the fear of the outcome is mitigated, so is the influence.

Fear of Retribution

Much of society's ability to function effectively can be traced to fear of retribution. It forms the basis of our system of laws and governmental policies. Why not drive 25 miles per hour above the posted speed limit? It's because you realize that you may get a ticket and fine for going that fast.

Managers use fear of retribution all the time. Policies are developed and disseminated that describe work hours, rules for achieving expectations, and production goals. For the most part, if the imposed requirement or action falls within the value system of the group or society, people will accept it and comply. The two factors that drive effectiveness are whether the requirement makes sense and the perception of how probable it is to be discovered in non-compliance.

Let's return to the speeding scenario as an example. Imagine that you are traveling down a very desolate portion of the interstate highway in the middle of Montana at 3:00 a.m. in the morning and the road is very straight all the way to the horizon. The speed limit is posted as 70 miles per hour. How many of us would be tempted to reach speeds of 80, 90, or even 100 miles per hour under those circumstances?

Change the scene to one where you are still on the interstate, but instead it's on the straight stretch between Los Angeles and San Diego and it is 2:00 p.m. on a Saturday. How much are you willing to go over the speed limit now?

The fear of retribution is used to influence our behavior all the time, but it is usually only effective to make people perform to some minimum. It is not an effective means to develop high-performance organizations or groups. Again, when the fear of retribution is eliminated so, too, is the influence.

Withholding

I can influence you by withholding something that you desire. My parents frequently used this technique: "You can't go out and play unless your room is clean," "You can't go with your friends until your homework is done," and many other withholding scenarios were used to influence me. I'm guessing your parents may have done the same thing. I have seen managers use this. Have you ever been presented with the situation that you don't get paid until the job is done? If you are a consultant, this is your life. Companies use this all the time to guarantee a certain quality or quantity.

Withholding can be effective, but at best it gets people to some minimum level of performance. If the minimum is all that you are after, then withholding could meet your needs.

Neglect/Ignoring

When you use neglect or ignoring as a tool to influence, you are isolating that resource from your group or organization. This technique is used when a manager wants to marginalize a person or group. It is the passive form of marginalization. The problem is that the outcome may not always be what you wanted. This type of behavior can result in two major effects – the person/group goes away or they rebel in such a way that you can no longer ignore them.

While you can influence using this technique, the results are never good for achieving highly effective organizations or groups.

Discrimination

Discrimination as used in this discussion is treating a person or group differently due to a physical or philosophical attribute (as opposed to some performance criteria). Discrimination can take two forms – discrimination for and against. A person can use discrimination to influence others. The person or group can be influenced one way or the other based upon whether the discrimination is in their favor or not. When a person discriminates against another person or group, it has the effect of isolating and minimizing them. They will probably leave or rise up to be heard and complain. If the discrimination is for the person or group, they may react favorably and see this discrimination as a reward for their behavior.

An example of discrimination can be to assign all the Jewish and Muslim people to work on Christmas Day while giving the Christian people the day off. While this may seem like a reasonable idea, it is actually detrimental to the group by introducing a facet of division. Do you give Hanukah off for the Jewish people? How about Ramadan for the Muslim people? People start to see others being treated differently and want what they perceive as equal treatment, which is a rather nebulous concept that is almost impossible to implement. So even when done with good intentions, discrimination usually introduces factors that are unforeseen and detrimental.

Favoritism

There are fine lines that distinguish some of these methods, and favoritism is one of them. Favoritism is the preferential treatment of various members or groups, and it is a subset of discrimination. The preferential treatment can be based upon familiarity, family relationships, school affiliation, or prior experience. Giving people or a group preferential treatment sets up an us-and-them division in the organization which is usually not a desirable outcome. Even if you set this up based upon performance, it will divide the group.

Sometimes the best of intentions can backfire and cause more harm than good. Instead of favoritism, when we look at the tools that we can use to influence people and groups, we will look at appreciation.

Pacification

"The customer is always right" is a common way to placate or pacify others. But as a tool to influence, this is also a dangerous method to employ. Agreeing to whatever certain people want is one way to clearly show people how to behave and what is acceptable. I have seen this used when people talk to customers and clients. While it is generally good to pacify a customer, it is more important to stick to the morals and values of the organization.

When pacification is used on members of the group, others and the person being pacified may think that this is a cultural norm. It soon becomes the norm for how people get what they want. As seen from the manager's perspective, it may be avoiding confrontation and a way to move on from the current situation. But pacifying as a tool for influence is not one that will create an environment of high performance or challenge. In fact, pacification places others in charge, negating any role of the leader.

Devaluing/Marginalizing

When we devalue or marginalize a person or group, we make a comparison that places them in a light that is not flattering or is even derogatory. Examples of this are Hitler's portrayal of the Jews, many coaches in how they describe other teams, and how politicians sometimes talk about their opposition. I have seen this tool used innocently by managers when they describe the organization's competition. "They can't possibly be as good as we are," is a statement that I have heard used.

This technique for influencing the perceptions of others always places someone as the inferior and places someone as the superior. It presumes inferiority and is a direct representation of a leader's morals and values. Many companies have made the mistake of characterizing their competition in this light, only to be beaten by them.

For the most part, organizations that use negative influence processes have limited effectiveness over time. This is because when the situation causing the negative influence is removed, so too is the motivation. Negative influence for the most part provides only a temporary motivation, but can cause long-term effects in the ability of leadership to influence by any other means. People have very long memories when they are affected by negative influencing.

The opposite of these methods, of course, are positive influencing tools. They have a tendency to motivate way beyond the time that the tool is actually used -- in some cases even to the point of the influence lasting for multiple generations. Positive influence lives in the realm of dreams and hope, which can last for a very long time.

Positive Influence Tools

Appreciation

Every human being on this planet needs appreciation. It is a universal need. It doesn't matter what race, culture, generation, or geographical location you are from; appreciation is a universal influencer. The trick is to determine what each person wants to be appreciated for and how they want to be appreciated.

Leaders use appreciation to influence people to continue behaviors that support their mission and vision. There are many ways to show appreciation, and good leaders make it a habit to appreciate as many people as possible. A leader knows that without people doing great things, nothing is accomplished. Leaders can influence others just by offering a simple "thank you" or by taking the time to listen. Appreciation doesn't always have to take center stage, but it doesn't hurt.

Quick Caveat: False appreciation or appreciation that is perceived as insincere or misguided can cause as much or more damage than not recognizing that appreciation is needed. But when done sincerely and timely, appreciation can motivate a person for a lifetime and serve as an example to others. My advice to leaders and would-be leaders is to find a way to appreciate someone for something every day either as a group or individually. Teach future leaders how to appreciate and it will serve them for a lifetime too.

> *"I guess we all like to be recognized not for one piece of fireworks, but for the ledger of our daily work."*
>
> *Neil Armstrong*

Visioning

Visioning is a technique used to articulate a specific desired future state in the minds of individuals or groups.

"Good business leaders create a vision, articulate the vision, passionately own the vision, and relentlessly drive it to completion."

Jack Welch

A vision of the future can be an extremely powerful influence. People have even given their lives in furtherance of their vision of the future while others are inspired to dedicate their entire lives to the effort. It is said that all great things are actually built twice, once in the mind and once in the world. We envision future states all the time. It is our primary way of navigating through this world and one of the ways that we make what we desire come true. All progress is made through this process of envisioning and doing.

One of the leader's primary responsibilities is to provide that vision of the future. If you don't do this, others will do it for you. People in the organization will develop their own personal visions of the future, which can cause competition for resources and create disjointed priorities and unfocused efforts.

The opposite is true for leaders who are successful in articulating a compelling vision. The clarity an articulated vision provides to the people in the organization creates the synergy that leaders prize so highly. But when you create a vision and articulate it, you must make sure that it is a vision that will last because a vision of the future that constantly changes can cause apathy and, worse, loss of confidence in the leadership.

Hope

Hope is one of the universal traits that make humans human. It is that belief in the notion that a situation will become more favorable or better in the future. Every person hopes for something in their lives. We all hope for better lives for ourselves and our children. We hope that our dreams or visions will come true. We rely on this hope as we experience the various trials of our lives.

A leader is a dealer in hope.

Napoleon Bonaparte

Leaders can influence and inspire with hope. By creating visions of the future, appreciating great efforts, offering rewards, and being examples, we create hope in the minds of our followers. Hope can be based on near-term or long-term desires for the future. The common denominator that helps hope to occur is a desired future state. Leaders have the opportunity to create hope and, by doing so, can create very powerful, long-lasting influence.

By Example

We also influence people by our actions. Leaders are examples of what people can become and how they should act. We can influence the cleanliness of a facility just by bending over and picking up a stray gum wrapper in the hallway. This act tells others that cleanliness is important and no one is beneath cleaning up. This influence can be persistent and powerful.

Martin Luther King, Jr., became the example of peaceful demonstration against unequal treatment of different races in America, but even he had a leader to follow, namely, Rosa Parks. Great leaders can come from anywhere. When I think of great examples of leadership by example, I think of a man whose identity we still do not know, and yet he became one of the most influential people of the 20th century.

Photo: *Associated Press*

Simply known as "Tank Man," his actions and bravery by standing up to a line of tanks has inspired millions to challenge oppression and hope for something better. Examples can be very powerful influencers. Never underestimate their power or fail to take the opportunity to be a great example.

Inspiration

Inspiration is motivation caused by a vision of a future state, an example, or compelling situation which calls to action the person or group. Examples can be everything from a child trying to be good in anticipation of appreciation from a parent, scenes of tranquility and peace, scenes of disaster or impending danger, and dreams of becoming a great leader.

> *"Our chief want is someone who will inspire us to be what we know we could be."*
>
> *Ralph Waldo Emerson*

Great leaders have learned to inspire by the stories they tell, the visions they have, and their actions as examples to others.

Inspiration can be used to influence people and this influence can be very long-lasting. Inspiration can cross generations. We have seen inspirational themes and ideas last centuries.

Managers direct and monitor, but leaders inspire. Learn what inspires people and you will have engaged their hearts and minds. Even if you can only inspire a small group of people, great things can happen.

> *"Never doubt that a small group of thoughtful, committed citizens can change the world. Indeed, it is the only thing that ever has."*
>
> *Margaret Mead*

Story Telling

Leaders influence us by telling and re-telling inspiring stories. From fables to parables to historical incantations, leaders use stories to provide examples of what to do, how to live, what not to do, and what can be done.

An example of one story that President Truman liked to tell was about his going to a Ku Klux Klan meeting with his friend Eddie Jacobson, who happened to be Jewish. President Truman relates that there had been death threats against him from the Klan and that he wanted to put an end to it. He decided that directly confronting the situation would be the best way to solve it.

He tells of the harrowing experience of going to the meeting, not knowing exactly what would happen, and addressing them and their activities as cowardly and shameful. He also relates that he lost that election, but never felt better about losing something in his life.

Another story of President Truman deals with his first job in a druggist's shop, and the two-faced actions that some people would have when they would publicly shout about the evils of alcohol but secretly drink for medicinal purposes. He used this story to explain the basis of his very straightforward and honest ways. He used to say, "I never did give anybody hell. I just told the truth and they thought it was hell."

President Ronald Reagan would often tell stories in his meetings and during conferences. Most of his stories were not long, but they effectively delivered his point. For example:

"How do you tell a communist? Well, it's someone who reads Marx and Lenin. And how do you tell an anti-communist? It's someone who understands Marx and Lenin."

Because President Reagan was the oldest president we ever had, he would often make light of it in the stories he told. Here's another:

"One of my favorite quotations about age comes from Thomas Jefferson. He said that we should never judge a president by his age, only by his work. And ever since he told me that, I've stopped worrying. And just to show you how youthful I am, I intend to campaign in all 13 states."

President Reagan's stories put people at ease, placed them on notice about his values, and connected him to the general population. You may not have agreed with him, but you probably believed he was genuine.

Storytelling can influence us by engaging our hearts and minds. They help us to relate to and support the vision or concept being shown to us or they help us understand different perspectives. Either way, we learn from stories, and that is what helps influence us. Considering their longevity and ability to mold and influence people, a story can be a very powerful tool in the hands of a skillful leader.

Rewards

I have included rewards because it is a form of positive influence, but at best it is only short term. Rewards are desired things that people get when they accomplish some task or reach a particular goal. Once they have the rewards, however, the influence is no longer applicable. Managers are more inclined to use rewards to influence people; leaders are more likely to use tools that engage people's hearts and minds, but they do use rewards as a way to appreciate people.

———————————————————

Influence is the tool of the leader and manager. Again, we actually cannot control very much at all, but we can influence people to action. Depending on the way we influence and what we do with that influence, we can either inspire people to accomplish great things or cause people to distrust us.

The other thing to remember is that any tool that is used to influence people is subject to the person or group's interpretation of the tool and its purpose. If they see it was done in good faith and for a good intention, then people generally accept the influence and comply with the wishes of the leader.

Influence and Manipulation

Many times I have been asked whether we are just using influence to manipulate people to do what we desire and to this I say, as a manager, yes, absolutely. One definition of "manipulation" is "skillful or artful management" (www.dictionary.com). Manipulation has an undesirable connotation, but it is what we are doing when we manage people. In its simplest terms, we are using influence to get people to do what we desire. Many times manipulation is associated with unfair situations, and I would say that this is often true. First epiphany managers use this all the time in the do-it-this-way-or-I'll-fire-you situation. Regardless of how you think about it, having the power to threaten your financial well-being is pretty much an unfair situation and many managers use it to their advantage.

On the other hand, a 4th epiphany leader uses influence to get you to realize that your current situation is not as desirable as some possible future state. While not an unfair tactic because it doesn't threaten to take anything from you, it nonetheless can be very powerful and motivating. Is this manipulation? In a way it is. As the leader, we build visions of what could or should be and in doing so devalue your present situation. The hope is that the difference in your realization is motivating. The *threat,* if there is one, comes from some external source (the other group, company, economy, etc.)

I view manipulation and influence as a spectrum. On one end of the spectrum of influence are threats and manipulation; on the other end of the spectrum are hope and inspiration. They are all forms of influence. If the influence is gained by threats of taking something from you, then it's probably manipulation; if the influence is gained by articulated desires of intangibles like hope, fairness, equality, freedom, or preservation of something of great value to society, it is normally inspiring.

When I think of manipulation, the Roman idea of decimation comes to mind. Talk about influence, if you or any of the men in your group show any form of cowardice, one in ten was executed by the other nine along with the leader. Those Romans had a way with influence. On the other end of the spectrum, I think of Dr. Martin Luther King's "I have a dream" speech. No threats, just a vision for the future and admonishment of the current situation. His influence is still felt today over 50 years later.

> *"I have a dream that one day this nation will rise up and live out the true meaning of its creed: "We hold these truths to be self-evident: that all men are created equal."*

> *Dr. Martin Luther King, Jr.*

The Influence Epiphany's Effect on Behavior

While this epiphany may happen at any point after a person becomes a manager/leader, it is normally associated with the growth seen in 3rd and 4th epiphany managers and leaders. The most dramatic changes in behavior would be evident in the 1st or 2nd epiphany managers, with the least noticeable changes in the 3rd and 4th epiphany managers/leaders.

So when a person has this epiphany, what behavior changes do we see? The answer is not as easy as with some of the other epiphanies. In some circumstances we don't see much of a difference and in other circumstances we see great changes. Let's look at each of the four epiphanies and see what happens.

The 1st epiphany manager's entire world and management style focuses on control. So for the most part, they believe that they have control and that "influence" is just a nicer word for controlling people. When they realize that they actually don't have control but only influence, they choose influences that have the greatest effect in getting people to do exactly what they want them to do. These are normally the threatening or withholding types of behaviors. They still expect that they can find that unfair advantage to hold over people so that they can have the most effective influence possible.

The 2nd epiphany manager still focuses on control, but, more to the point, it is control within preset boundaries. So if a 2nd epiphany manager comes to realize this epiphany, their behavior will tend toward influencing with reward programs and other incentives; but they will still employ a fair amount of dissuaders in the form of withholding and discrimination. The realization that control doesn't exist actually works to support this second epiphany.

A 3rd epiphany manager will normally already have this epiphany or will realize it shortly after having the third epiphany. When they have this epiphany about influence, their behavior usually starts to include empathy. They start to use appreciation (listening, thanking, and recognition) and visioning to influence.

A 4th epiphany leader will normally have realized the epiphany about influence by this time, but as they realize it, their behavior tends to move more toward inspirational motivational techniques. They will inspire with hope, vision, and personal example. It is rare to have a 4th epiphany leader that doesn't either understand or innately know the truth about this realization.

Leading Even When You Are No Longer Around

One of the hallmarks of effective leaders is that their influence persists beyond their office and in some cases their lives. When you think of truly effective leaders, those that gather huge momentum in people and ideals, their leadership legacy persists (and not all are good legacies). When we think of effective leaders, they influenced us with very powerful visions and emotions. From the truly great – Gandhi, Martin Luther King, Jr., Ronald Reagan, and Steve Jobs – to the heinous – Hitler, Osama Bin Laden, and Bernie Madoff – they were all extremely influential in their causes. With the heinous, we now know what to constantly stay alert for and hopefully will not fall under the influence of such again. With the great, we memorialize them and their visions for the future.

Effective leaders are not great in and of themselves. They coax that great energy and belief in our abilities from us. John Buchan said it best, "The task of leadership is not to put greatness into humanity, but to elicit it, for the greatness is already there." With the tools of influence, they get us to believe in ourselves, the vision of what could be, and inspire us to become great. They do this by sometimes showing us what we can do in their examples.

"One man with courage makes a majority."

Andrew Jackson

As a leader, never underestimate what the effect that a single courageous action can have for the present and the future. Rosa Parks is a modern-day example of a single courageous act that still influences our thinking, our laws, and our national values; and I suspect that it will have influence for some time in the future. Other examples can be traced back thousands of years to the stories of King David in the Old Testament. To this day, we can see how these stories apply to our lives. They still influence us powerfully. What stories do you want told and how do you want to influence the future?

"The key to successful leadership today is influence, not authority."

Ken Blanchard

Understanding Influence, A Vital Epiphany

Chapter 7

How Leaders Affect Organizational Environment

Without a doubt, leaders of organizations affect the people they lead or manage. In this chapter, however, I want to take the time to explore how what we do as leaders affect the groups or organizations we lead. This is a general discussion that can be applied to all levels of managers and leaders, and hopefully you will find how it can apply to your own situation.

Why do leaders have such an effect on their organizations? To answer that question, we need to look at basic human nature and social development. Humans are social creatures. We are born into a social unit, we live in social units, and we work in social units. This natural need for social units is also reinforced by what seems to be an innate need for appreciation. Another factor that should be considered is the human need to survive, which manifests itself in the form of hope. Each of these situations and traits play into the reasons why leaders can have such an effect on organizations.

The social aspect of our human development drives us to join and identify with groups. We find our need for security and appreciation in these groups. The instinct for survival is a little more complicated and consists of two parts: the physical needs and the psychological needs. To survive, you need to satisfy both. As far as the specifics around the physical needs, those are easy to identify – food, water, air, and shelter form the basics.

When you examine the psychological needs of people, you find that appreciation and hope are required. Without hope, people give up and will not survive. Hope is the desire for a better – or at least the same – future state. The person who can articulate this hope of a desired future state for a group becomes the leader. Napoleon got it right when he said that leaders are dealers in hope.

In addition to that, leaders hold the capability to provide appreciation. The person who can articulate a desired vision and provide appreciation will become the leader even if they have not been appointed to the position of leader.

This ability to articulate a vision and provide appreciation is one of the reasons that leaders fail or succeed. It is also one of the reasons that I believe that leadership can be a learned skill. While not every person who does this will become a great leader, they are required skills. The primary reason people don't become leaders is that their vision is not widely accepted by the group. Some people are just not motivated or inspired by "increasing shareholder value."

So leaders become effective in affecting groups through their visions and how they appreciate the group, and both are tied to basic human needs. But it is more complex than just that. Because they have become the leader, there is a certain authority that is granted to them by the group. This authority can be simply granted or it can be earned. It is a natural reaction of the people in the group to recognize this authority and give deference to it and to the leader as a result. They have needs for appreciation (from the leader and group) and want to understand their part in making the vision happen.

Many people in the group have hope that they too will become leaders, and they may use this person as their example or pathway to get there. They want to understand how and why this person became the leader. All of this can combine to cause people in the group to focus on the leader. With this focus, the effects of appreciation, leading by example, and causing inspiration are multiplied. The net effect is that whatever a leader does will have an effect on the group.

Let's explore what some of the reactions from a leader's words and actions can accomplish and how they affect the organization. Remember that, even though these are common observations, they do seem to follow a predictable pattern – however, they may not cause the same results in your situation. As an example, stealing may be considered a necessary rite of passage in a street gang; but in most other organizations, stealing would be considered a heinous act worthy of group expulsion. So, specific acts and words can mean different things to different people at different times.

(*My catchy disclaimer:* "Your mileage may vary.")

What My Words Can Do

Words can be very powerful depending on who says them, the subject, amount of emotional attachment, and perspective presented. Leaders already have a power position with authority already granted to them which makes it assured that their words will be heard and evaluated.

By Our Information

We provide information to the group or organization. What we tell people can cause a variety of reactions from panic to apathy, even feelings of security and a wide range of other feelings.

When we provide information can be just as important as what is said. Think about when you give a group good news or bad news. Which do you give on a Friday and which do you give on a Tuesday? Why? Many experts say that the end of the week is the best time to deliver company-wide bad news. The reasoning is that people can have the weekend to consider the situation rather than acting on it emotionally during the work week. Good news, however, can and should be delivered anytime that it is learned.

By and large, groups look forward to information coming from their leader. They experience communication from the leader as validation of their work, their feelings for the organization, and the organization's progress. It gives the perception that leadership is trying to stay in touch with everyone. These days, information can be disseminated quite frequently and in any number of ways; and when thoughtfully implemented, these information sessions can be an effective means of connecting with an organization. Presidents Roosevelt and Reagan didn't have the communication tools we enjoy today, but they kept in touch quite effectively, nevertheless, with their discussions and addresses to the nation. Using tones and phrases that one would use for friends, leaders can build a relationship with their audience. Making sure that there is a reliable frequency in these communiqués is an important aspect of relationship-building as well.

Leaders need to decide how much detail they share in their information briefings. As to whether more detail is better, that depends on your audience. Another consideration should be the perspective your audience holds about the subject and the effect that this perspective has upon how the information will be understood and viewed. Social and cultural norms also affect the way information is understood and viewed. So leaders must be sensitive to how their language could affect their message. Will the images that you wish to convey be represented in the intended manner when people consider your words?

Does what we say give the perception that we, as leaders, have listened, appreciated, and validated the issues of the audience? Even when we speak to our groups or organizations, we can make it a quasi two-way conversation. When we address the issues and concerns of our audience, we make a connection with them and validate their beliefs that the leadership is a part of the team and in this situation with them.

One of the most important communication techniques we can use to affect our organizations is to teach people. When we teach people, provide them with new information that helps them perform a task, or give them understanding of a situation, we gain their respect. We must understand the material enough to teach it and enough to answer questions. But when we do, we become a group expert on that subject. Recognized expertise on subjects is another way leaders gain respect. It also helps support the perception that the leader has the ability to make good decisions.

The information we give and, just as importantly, how we deliver it can be very effective in building and maintaining our influence over groups of people. But when information is delivered ineffectively, the message can be misconstrued and potentially damage the leader's reputation and influence. Leaders need to truly understand this relationship and become experts in how delivering information affects the formation of influence.

By Our Requests

Look up the definition of request, and you will see that it is simply asking someone to do something. A request does not actually require compliance or even consideration; but when a request comes from a leader, it can take on a more significant meaning, to the point of becoming a directive or even a quest.

How Leaders Affect Organizational Environment

Up until November 6, 1919, Albert Einstein's theory of relativity was the subject of fierce debate among scientists, and he diligently sought to find definitive proof that his theories were correct. Sir Frank Watson Dyson had devised an experiment that would prove one of the major aspects of Einstein's theory, but Einstein was not able to undertake the experiment himself. He requested help from the scientific community, and various people took up the challenge. The story of how Arthur Eddington proved what we now know as gravitational lensing is epic and serves as a true example of how a simple request can become a quest for many committed individuals.

Why does this occur? What is it about a simple request that can cause a company or organization to change its direction and even mission to accomplish it? A request is seen as helping the leader or cause. Depending on the status and deference given the leader, a request can mean different things to different people and groups. To illustrate the point, imagine how easily a simple request from my mother to clean up my room would have gotten lost among the other things that occupied my mind at age 12. Then imagine a situation where the president of the nation requests that I research a certain situation. Why might I spend the next 48 hours straight and all my resources at hand doing nothing else but to satisfy this request? Why the difference?

In all the cultures I have studied, not complying with a request from the leader can be construed as a sign of disrespect for the person, the position that they represent, or the group that they represent. For the most part, people see the leader as the embodiment of the organization or group that they lead; so not complying with the leader's request is like not complying with a request from the group. After all, the leaders wouldn't have asked us if they didn't need it; right?

Leaders need to understand the impact that simple requests can have on their groups. They need to understand that their request represents a request from the organization. When completed, the request would benefit the organization or the leader's ability to make decisions that affect the organization. Recognizing this perception can help one understand why a request is a very powerful influencing tool.

By Our Orders

An order is a command to do some action. When a leader gives an order, they expect it to be followed. Followers know that orders address something important and that orders are very important. Orders are not optional; they must be complied with. Not following an order from the leader is tantamount to treason within the group's culture. Not complying with an order can be seen as a sign of disrespect to the leader, to the group, and the culture.

Most effective leaders that I have studied almost never give orders. Leaders know that requests have almost just as much impact and influence. When an order must be given, then, it is for immediacy and is vital that the action take place for the well-being of the organization or the safety of its people. People respond to orders from the leader in various ways, but they almost always respond by complying with them.

Orders can be very influential in their aftermath. That is, when they are issued, they will be complied with; but the results of the order may be considered by the organization for a long time after the event that occasioned the order. Was the order needed? Did it allow us to respond appropriately to the situation? The group's or organization's answers to these questions will determine whether a leader's actions were correct and build or destroy their influence. The fact that orders will be judged post-

situation is a powerful reason for leaders to carefully consider how they use their ability to influence – especially since predicting an outcome is so difficult to do.

By Our Stories

Stories are words that tell us about a situation, the actions taken, and the results – and they are among the most powerful influencers. The most influential stories are those that paint vivid images that the audience can relate to. If people can relate and have personal ties to the situations being described, they become personal. In this way, a leader can literally talk to millions of people and make a very personal connection with many of them. Presidents Reagan and Truman were experts at this.

Dan Rather, a long-time reporter at CBS News, said that if Hollywood taught Mr. Reagan anything, it was the value of a good story – and a good punch line. Reagan used his stories to connect examples of values to the actions of the people he was addressing. He used them to provide examples of what we can become and to inspire action toward that goal.

Great leaders have this in common: They can tell stories that preserve the time-honored values they wish to perpetuate. The stories they tell convey what is important to the leader. By selecting situations many have experienced and truths which relate to their audience, they can illustrate the views they believe their audience should adopt.

Stories convey thoughts that inspire us, provide good and bad examples, and are used to appreciate people and their efforts. What stories have you told? What results did you get? Were they helpful in achieving your goals? Did the audience relate to the story?

I highly recommend the use of stories to build and maintain influence. They address not only the needs of the mind, but of the heart as well.

The words of a leader are the tools they use to place images in the mind and passions in the heart. We all have access to the same words. It's how we use them to inspire when we issue a call to action that makes us leaders. Consider how the following words and advice are used and how you can shape your words to do the same:

> *"If you want to build a ship, don't drum up people to collect wood and don't assign them tasks and work, but rather teach them to long for the endless immensity of the sea."*
>
> Antoine de Saint-Exupery

What My Actions Can Do

Actions send messages in a couple of different ways – they can be examples of what people should be doing, they can cause others to react, and they can cause others to consider the values driving those actions. I keep harping on the fact that leaders are constantly under the microscope of their group's scrutiny, and that's because *every action will have meaning to someone*. Every action will have some response, whether immediate or delayed, and leaders need to be aware that their actions can influence greatly the perception of the group. A leader's actions may actually determine whether that leader will be successful and effective or not. So let's look at what your actions can accomplish.

By Leading

> *"Men make history and not the other way around.*
> *In periods where there is no leadership, society*
> *stands still. Progress occurs when courageous,*
> *skillful leaders seize the opportunity to change*
> *things for the better."*
>
> *Harry Truman*

Leading is an action. You must take action to lead. You cannot lead sitting at a desk and pontificating about values or dreams. You must go out and lead whether that is talking to people in the field, evaluating a situation, or being at the front of the charge.

President Truman laid the groundwork for the civil rights that we have in this country when, even as a senatorial candidate, he stated "I believe in the brotherhood of man, not merely the brotherhood of white men, but the brotherhood of all men before law. I believe in the Constitution and the Declaration of Independence. In giving the Negroes the rights which are theirs, we are only acting in accord with our own ideals of a true democracy." Remember that this was said in 1940 in a state that was considered southern during the Civil War.

During the Democratic Convention, President Truman passed a civil rights platform and made essentially the same speech that President Roosevelt had made. In response to this, Governor Strom Thurmond and several other Southern delegates left the convention. When a reporter asked the Governor why he left the convention when President Truman's words were virtually the same as President Roosevelt's, Thurmond's reply was "Yes – but Truman really means it." We lead by our actions. Our actions are simply our way of following through on our values, intentions, and promises. President Truman had a reputation of follow-through and for unwavering values.

Leaders set a course and follow it. They define the vision and take action to obtain that vision. They gain influence, trust, and a reputation based upon the actions they take toward those goals. Actions that don't help the organization reach the vision or actions that cannot be perceived as helping reach the vision diminish a leader's effectiveness and influence. The actions a leader takes that clearly support the achievement of the vision or goal is what bolsters respect, loyalty, and trust.

I can't tell you what specific actions will help you gain influence, trust, or respect; but I believe these general guidelines will help you achieve the stature of a leader. People and organizations expect that a leader will lead. When the leader fails to lead, they lose faith in the vision and the person at the same time. This loss of trust can occur very quickly. And interestingly, it can be built and established just as fast. Doing nothing is not an option. Doing nothing causes disenchantment with the leader. It creates doubt about their ability to reach the vision and sets the example of apathy in the organization. As the leader, if you don't know what to do, ask. Someone will offer assistance; the people in your organization have just as much at stake with your success as you do.

Leadership is an action. As they say at Nike, "Just do it."

By Example

There is probably no more powerful organizational influencer than the actions of its leader. Throughout this book, I have given examples of great leaders. And their great success is that they led by their example. Whether it was Gandhi going on a hunger strike, Theodore Roosevelt leading the charge up San Juan Hill, Harry Truman confronting the Ku Klux Klan, or Steve

Jobs refusing to compromise on the user experience, these leaders became the examples that they had to be in order to further their beliefs and visions.

Under the organizational microscope, a leader's example can have magnified effects. When one person sees something that they believe is a good example, I suspect they tell a few people. Then as this process is repeated, many learn of the leader's action. The same thing happens when a leader sets a bad example, but I suspect the effect is even greater. There has been research that when people have a good experience, they tell four or five people; but when they have a bad experience, they tell ten or more. You can imagine how this phenomenon works with leadership examples.

Because a leader's behavior serves as an example to their followers, a great opportunity exists for a leader to influence their group through their actions. Not all actions need to be public displays. In fact, some of the most effective actions can occur with just a few people observing. Looking back at the example of Rosa Parks, I doubt that she had much of an audience when she refused to give up her seat on that bus, yet her actions led to a tremendous resurgence in the civil rights movement which eventually brought cultural change to our society.

It is said that the measure of a man's values occurs in their actions when there is no one there to see them. In today's world, it is actually rare that a leader is not being observed. Picking up that garbage in the parking lot when no one is around might seem like an unseen action, but imagine the several people who can see that parking lot from their windows or the security team that observes through the security cameras. You actually never know who is watching and what they will do with that knowledge. Leaders, live your life as if it were on the front page of the "*New York Times*," because it could be.

I leave this section with a thought from Machiavelli, the consummate observer of human interaction:

"A return to first principles in a republic is sometimes caused by the simple virtues of one man. His good example has such an influence that the good men strive to imitate him, and the wicked are ashamed to lead a life so contrary to his example."

Niccolo Machiavelli

By Appreciating

Appreciation is one of the universal motivators. It works for everyone. As a leader, you just need to find out how and for what people want to be appreciated. I have discussed appreciation previously in this book, but here are the specific effects to the organization.

When you privately show appreciation for a person, as with your examples, they tell people about it. People learn of your ability to see what individuals do and they develop the perception that you will see what they do and maybe show appreciation for them too. This perception can spread very quickly as you show appreciation for people and their effort. This is why I say that, as a leader, you should find something to appreciate every day in your group or organization. It doesn't have to be a public spectacle and, in many ways, the private shows of appreciation can have the deepest meaning and have the longest-lasting effects.

In many ways, organizations in our modern societies have come to expect that our leaders will have some form of public appreciation for certain groups or people. It's almost an expectation that there will be some kind of annual award meeting or gathering. This is why I push the daily private shows of appreciation. They are unexpected and it shows your people that what they do is important and helps the organization reach its goals. To do this private appreciating, the leader must get out into the organization and observe. They must actually search out situations and actions that need praise and support.

"It is amazing what you can accomplish if you do not care who gets the credit."

Harry S. Truman

You can see from this quote that appreciation needs to go to those who need it. Different people need different levels of appreciation to feel that they are contributing significantly to the organization's goals and vision. It is up to you as the leader to determine who and how much appreciation you show. Teach your leadership team and managers how to appreciate people. Teach your leadership that it's not what the leader/manager accomplishes, but rather what their teams accomplish. Leadership is about the team's accomplishments, not the leaders'. Too often we focus on the leader's contribution and not what the group did to accomplish it and this focus on the leader can have detrimental effects. People can develop the perception that no matter what they do, the leader/manager will get the credit and rewards. This is a very de-motivating situation for the group. Make sure that groups are appreciated for the accomplishments just as much or more than the leadership/management.

As you can see, your actions as a leader can and do have a great effect on the organization's overall perspective and motivation. In so many words, the leader's actions and words influence the group to the point that one could say that you control the group's perspective and motivation level. But as we have already discussed, control is an illusion; yet influence can be very powerful indeed.

Action and Reaction – Organizational Laws

In Chapter 1, I discussed how we could benefit by applying Newton's law of action and reaction to organizations. Remember that Newton's third law of motion, simply stated, is that for every action there is an opposite and equal reaction. The same principle applies to organizations, just not in equality or opposition. In many cases, an action on the part of the leader can multiply exponentially in its effect. A single action can change an entire organization's culture or direction.

With all actions there will be a reaction; however, because of the complexities of human interaction, they are hard to predict. So this relationship got me to think about how the natural laws of physics could be quite applicable in some form to organizational and sociological situations. I, therefore, decided to include them as something that a leader can use to understand and predict responses by the organization.

Newton's Third Law of Motion

Newton's third law of motion is translated as: "To every action there is always opposed an equal reaction." This law has a direct application to organizational dynamics. In our arena, it can be stated in this way:

Newton's Third Law As Applied To Organizations

Any action by a leader will have an effect on the organization.

Notice that I stated "*any action*." Whether it is deciding to ignore that gum wrapper in the hallway, making a company-wide speech, or volunteering for a community event, people from your organization are watching, learning, and considering your actions. The actions that you take can be multiplied exponentially or appear to be ignored. In reality, your actions are never ignored but are, rather, kept as examples of how people should act, used as validation of their perception of you, copied, or acted upon in a myriad of other ways.

Using this organizational law as a predictor is not really possible with the limited information stated here; but with an understanding of your organization's values and culture and with experience, it is possible to determine or assume some common reactions. Remember that you are trying to predict the actions of a group of individuals. People may not have the same reaction; in fact, I can guarantee that they won't. The value of this law is that you realize that you will get a reaction from everything you do as a leader.

Second Law of Thermodynamics

In the physical process of transferring energy from a source to a different receiver, there is always a loss out of the system. This loss is called entropy. Basically, the second law of thermodynamics states that you cannot have a perfect transfer of energy; that you will always have losses and that, because of this, you cannot reverse the process without putting energy into the system. For those of you that have not studied physics, this is the real reason that you cannot make a perpetual motion machine. When I look at applying this law to organizations and leadership, it translates in several ways:

Second Law of Thermodynamics As Applied To Organizations

If the leadership doesn't constantly put energy into the organization, it will slowly quit making progress and eventually disorganize. Another

252

way to look at this is no leadership = no organization.

As organizations grow, the energy required to continue making progress also grows. This increased energy is due to losses caused by the formation of bureaucracy.

Long-term projects need new people from time to time to interject new energy into the project.

The takeaway for leaders is that you must find ways to remove the bureaucracy (energy-robbing processes) and interject new passion into the effort to reach your goals and vision. Adding more people to the organization can do it, but they have to have the passion and motivation to reach the goals and believe in the vision. This actually leads us to the next analogy.

Critical Mass

As a simple explanation, a self-sustaining nuclear reaction will not occur without a minimum level of nuclear reactive material being present. Less than this amount of nuclear reactive material and the reaction will cease. If there is more nuclear reactive material than is necessary, the reaction will continue and could accelerate. We call this amount of material where the nuclear reaction becomes self-sustaining "critical mass."

Another characteristic of this reaction is that if there is nothing to moderate or control the reaction, the reaction can accelerate exponentially. This would be an uncontrolled chain reaction which is usually associated with a tremendous output of energy. When this reaction is controlled, the energy produced and harnessed can be very impressive.

Let's take these ideas and use them to help us understand and influence organizations. If you think of what causes motivation and the associated action within an organization, you can identify four main components. The components are both specific to individuals and aggregated within the organizational environment.

The first is the *desirability of the vision or goals*. This is the personal acceptance of the vision or goal. If the desirability is high, there is a good chance that it will drive and create motivation within the individual.

The second is the *believability of the obtainment vision or goal*. If a person believes that they can obtain the goal or vision, they will evaluate the level of effort and make a value decision as to the benefits of obtainment.

The third component is the *perception of the role that the individual is to play in the obtainment of the vision*. If they feel that their participation is fundamental to the obtainment, their level of energy dedicated to the objective will be directly proportional to this perception of involvement. These three components combine to form an individual's passion for the obtainment of the vision or goal.

The fourth component is the *saturation level of acceptance*; that is, what percentage of people in the group has developed a passion for the vision and are motivated to action. This is a measurable characteristic of the organization.

So how does this concept of critical mass work within an organizational setting? It is this fourth component, the saturation level, which is the key to this concept. If enough of the people in the group have a passion for the vision, then by many different sociological processes, the group as a whole will gain energy and passion for the obtainment of the vision.

In all organizations there is a saturation level below which they will not obtain their goals. The same is not necessarily true for the opposite situation. Even if you have a 100 percent saturation of acceptance, it will not guarantee your organization's obtainment of the vision. The takeaway concept here is that, without the critical mass of saturation, the organization will fail to obtain its goals.

Another key to this can be derived from the first three components. Leaders can influence perceptions and therefore the desirability, belief in, and roles that people play in the vision or goals.

As a leader, you must inspire enough passion in enough people that you achieve critical mass and then allow the organization to use this energy and passion to achieve the vision. Be prepared for the organizational energy that can be generated and have a plan to use it effectively. Just like a nuclear reaction, the energy developed for the vision can grow exponentially.

Schrödinger's Cat

In quantum physics, there is a paradox that Austrian physicist Erwin Schrödinger described in a thought experiment. The paradox is illustrated by a cat within a sealed box and that at this time the cat can both be alive and dead. If a person opens the box, the cat then is only seen in the dead or alive state, not both, but while the box is unopened, the cat is both alive and dead. This thought experiment helps us understand that, in quantum physics, objects can and do exist in two different states at the same time. So how does this apply to organizations?

Think about an organization before there is interaction from the leader. The organization can exist in several states (effective, progressive, degenerative, focused, unfocused, etc.) and usually some form of all of the above. When a leader interacts with the organization, the people choose one of three states – aligned, non-aligned, or ambivalent. But just as when Schrödinger's cat's box is opened, the contents take on a specific state. The people will self-identify with, against, or be unconcerned with the leader's presence and actions. The interaction by the leader changes things, regardless of the action, time of interaction, or place/time.

In 1924, there were some studies performed at the Hawthorne Works plant at the Western Electric Company in Illinois. The sociologists were attempting to isolate factors that affect worker performance. They increased the lighting and productivity went up. Then they decreased the lighting and productivity went up again – which was exactly the opposite of what they expected. Why?

It happens that the workers were affected by the very presence of the investigators. This phenomenon is caused by the fact that someone was paying attention to the workers and asking their opinions. In essence, they saw this as appreciation of their opinions and concerns.

A leader, by their very presence, will cause an effect. What that effect is, you can influence; but if you are not there, then the organization can and will exist in many states. The takeaway is that, if you want to influence your organization, then you have to show up, open that box, and see what happens.

Boyle's Gas Law

Boyle's gas law deals with the relationship of pressure, temperature, and volume within a closed system. If you increase temperature and maintain the same volume, the pressure will increase. If you reduce the volume while maintaining the same temperature, the pressure will increase. Also, if you decrease the volume, pressure and temperature, both will go up, which is why diesel engines work. So how does this help us explain how organizations work?

Imagine that as the leader you can control the number of people in the organization (volume), the amount of work required to be done (temperature), and the schedule to which the work is to be accomplished (pressure). Let's put these elements into play to see how the concept works. If I increase the number of people and leave the schedule the same, the amount of work per person will go down. If I keep the number of people the same and decrease the schedule, the amount of work per person will go up.

Try it on your own and you will find that if you think about organizations in this manner that the variables of people, work, and schedule will follow Boyle's law in a relatively proportional way. You cannot calculate exact effects like you can with the physical world, but they can give a pretty good indication of what is happening in the organization.

―――――――――――――――――――――――――――――

These are just some of the correlations I have noticed between the world of physics and the world of sociology. There are actually many more. While there are no equations or models that can precisely predict an organization's behavior, we have become fairly adept at modeling some of the behaviors in certain situations and in certain societies. Dealing with people and organizations is never an exact science; but as with anything, as you gain experience with the group, you will gain insight into what the group values and then you will be able to better understand their reactions.

A leader's actions can influence and change the environments of organizations in very significant ways. Hopefully this chapter will give you some understanding of how that happens and what you can do to help the organization achieve the goals and vision that you set out.

A key philosophy that any leader must understand is that, only by changing themselves can they hope to change the organizations they lead. The changes you implement can and do have tremendous effects on an organization. Think of all the ways these epiphanies change you as you become a leader. Consider the changes that you make and how those changes could affect your group. What changes are you going to make today?

Chapter 8

Selection and Care of Prospective Leaders

A fellow manager asked me several years ago – okay, over 20 years ago – "What do we need to do to grow leaders in our organization?"

"Provide Miracle-Gro® and beer," was my tongue-in-cheek response. But the question stayed with me. It actually took me back to that place as a child when I began to wonder what made some people become great leaders who could mean so much to so many people. In a very real sense, this question put me back on the path to discover what it takes to become a great leader which gave rise to the ideas in this book.

So what does it take to grow a leader? How do we identify and help people become leaders? In the past, the selection of future managers and leaders was done by picking the best _____ in the department and promoting them. The best engineer, salesperson, technician, or line person was identified and promoted to supervisor or manager. Leaders were usually chosen from among the best managers. It was standard practice in almost every industry and human endeavor and is still in practice today. It may be appropriate in certain circumstances to select and promote supervisors and managers in this way. But having read this far, hopefully you now understand how ineffective this method is for selecting future leaders. In fact, it is probably one of the worst ways to identify and select prospective leaders.

Most organizations talk about training leaders, but what they really do is train managers. There is a true disconnect as to what real leadership is, what it will do for an organization, and how to find the right leader. Moreover, leaders are often misunderstood because they are agents of change and organizations naturally tend to resist change. But organizations, like any life form, must adapt to survive – and leaders recognize this. They naturally evolve in response to their changing environment and push their organizations to do the same. In fact, good leaders anticipate the changes that need to be made in order to adapt and survive. And the best leaders actually envision a future and then change whatever they need to in order to make that future come true.

The process these leaders go through may seem confusing, incongruous – even mysterious. Their organizations appear to exist in constant chaos. But for organizations that prefer stasis as opposed to progress, an environment of constant chaos is completely unacceptable. It is one of the reasons organizations prefer to train managers, since a manager will maintain an organization in relative stasis. But an organization that isn't moving forward is, in fact, falling behind.

It's important to understand that true leaders are difficult to deal with. They usually have a very unique way of looking at situations and the world. Their thoughts are uncommon, their methods may seem unconventional, and they fail frequently. If you are really serious about finding and growing true leaders, be prepared for the difficult road ahead for the potential leader, the organization, and their mentors. True leaders, if given the opportunity, can and will change the world as you know it – it's what they do, and it's not a bad legacy to be a part of.

Identification of Prospective Leaders

So how do you find great leaders? What are the characteristics that will guarantee success? Can you measure a person's potential?

This book proposes a different way to select people for prospective leadership positions. I want to describe a method that looks at the potential to acquire and develop the unique skills necessary for leadership. What we need is a way to identify the specific tendencies that provide the greatest potential to make it to the 4th epiphany. As you read about these tendencies, you will see how they mirror the fully developed traits found in 4th epiphany leaders. But the reality is that most people don't go on to become 4th epiphany leaders. Fully 80 percent stop at the 2nd or 3rd epiphanies. In fact, you may not recognize a great potential candidate for leadership in your midst if you base your selection upon the epiphanies alone.

We learn from our everyday experiences, and we develop and change every day. And that means that a person can develop these traits at any time. And the interesting thing is that very few of these traits are innate, which means that we can create environments to develop the traits that will assist us on our journey to becoming leaders. So let's put the path aside for just a moment to explore the underlying tendencies that must exist if you are to reach the 4th epiphany.

First and foremost,

- *They have the ability to tell great stories.*

They have the ability to form very vivid, shared images in the minds of others. This ability translates in a leader to being able to promulgate a vision for the future. Without this ability, a person can become a pretty good manager, but not a true leader.

The good news is that this can be taught; so if they don't have it initially, they must have the capability to learn it.

- *They have the ability to gain respect from people.*

However they do it – whether through their actions, ideas, or experiences – other people naturally trust them and go to them for their thoughts and opinions.

- *They are authentic.*

Being an authentic human is acting and behaving in accordance with your own deeply held values. These people do not check polls to tell them what they should think or how they should act. They are very much their own person. Being authentic doesn't mean that they are averse to change. Quite to the contrary, they are comfortable with change and they undertake change confidently knowing that their foundational values will serve as touchstones for guidance.

- *They like people.*

They are not necessarily extroverts – in fact, they may be quite introverted – but they like people and see potential in all people. People interest them. In rare instances, they will be natural-born leaders – those people who others will form around, listen to, and follow.

A word of caution about this tendency: In reality, this tendency is highly situational. In the absence of true leadership, people in need will follow anyone who presents a potential solution. I included it in the list because, if you can observe a person over a relatively long period of time and they continue to do this, then it can be a good indicator of potential success as a leader. And, of course, someone who answers a need may also continue on to fulfill whatever is lacking.

- *They take the roads less traveled.*

It would not be uncommon to find a potential leader that has a varied background, such as farmer, software programmer, and UNICEF volunteer. It would also not be uncommon to find that they travel and enjoy different cultures and their interaction. I look for the engineer that also took creative writing or media production as electives, as an example.

- *They question and are curious.*

They want to understand how things work. They ask why people act that way, and really want to know. Their quest for knowledge will commonly lead them outside of their chosen career paths. They want to know why certain cultures act the way they do. They will be eclectic to some degree.

- *They respect achievement, not words.*

While words create visions that inspire them, they have respect for achievement. It is not uncommon for them to ask, "What you have done lately?" Not that they don't respect your opinion or thoughts, but they will be more interested in what you have actually done. Their heroes will normally be people that did great things.

Lastly, but of vital importance, is;

- *They are passionate about learning.*

Not just the ability, or even the desire, but passion to learn and grow. These are the people that are willing to drink when we lead them to water. There is no question about it. They want to learn. They are lifelong learners; in fact, they will find ways to learn on their own.

This is what I look for in people that I believe have a good potential to be great leaders. Remember that I differentiate leaders from managers. A great manager might be the best engineer or technician, but great leaders require completely different skill sets and attitudes. As with anything that has to do with people, your mileage may vary. I know that it is not a guarantee that a person that exhibits all of these traits will be successful; but in my experience, they are great indicators. You may have developed your own list of tendencies and wish to combine those with some of mine. Regardless, finding people who have the potential to be great leaders is difficult at best, but the rewards of finding one has no upper limit as to what can happen.

Mentorship

The long road to becoming a leader is best when there is a guide and companion to travel with. That companion is a mentor. The mentor/mentored relationship is one that is chosen by both parties and needs to be based upon mutual respect.

I'm not sure how to convince someone they need a mentor, but I do know that all prospective leaders need one. Whether that relationship is initially assigned by someone in your organization or there is some type of meet and greet between prospective leaders and available mentors, the leader trainees need access to this type of resource.

Once a relationship is established, there are certain ground rules that need to be agreed to by both parties. Here are a few that I use:

- Honesty is expected.
- What is said between us is kept between us.

- Both are required to make the time. (How much time is agreed upon)

There is usually some kind of commitment by both to keep an open mind, but also to the level of work expected of both mentor and mentee. Both individuals must understand that this is an on-going, long-term relationship. Either can end the relationship if personal circumstances require it (e.g., the mentor was to become their direct boss, the prospective leader decides to pursue other paths, the mentor can no longer perform or keep their commitments). Mentorship is really a commitment between two people to help each other succeed.

Being a mentor is a lot like raising a child. You are dealing with someone who is learning new things, working in new environments, and having to learn different behaviors. More than likely, all of this will be very foreign to them. It's a lot like sending your child to school for the first time. One of the things that you must explain to them is that most everything they have learned in life no longer applies and that their environment will be entirely new, even if the location is one that they have been at for years.

As a mentor, like raising children, there will be wondrous moments and tragic situations. Remember that failure is a part of learning. Expect that the mentee will fail, and that you will have to be there for them to help them understand the failure and how to prevent it in the future. The key to success as a mentor is not giving up, even when you both want to. Most mentors that I have known are mentors for the rest of their lives. Certainly, the relationships you form with the mentored can last that long if you so desire.

"No one learns as much about a subject as one who is forced to teach it."

Peter F. Drucker

Teaching is an activity that benefits both teacher and student. As mentor, you will need to take on the role of teacher. Be observant, ask, and find out what your prospective leader needs to learn. It usually isn't hard to find something. I know from my own experiences being mentored and mentoring, the opportunities to teach come often; but as Mr. Drucker so eloquently pointed out, the teacher must have mastery over the material. Knowing this, I continually study, re-learn and expand my knowledge of new subjects all the time. In this way, teaching benefits both greatly.

What we teach is very important. As mentor, we should be teaching not what to think, but how to think. How do we help this prospective leader open their mind and see different realities, remembering that this is what causes people to have epiphanies?

Never forget that the bond between mentor and mentee is based upon trust and mutual respect. And never forget why we mentor – there is no greater legacy to leave. Consider what some teachers and their students have accomplished: Socrates had a student named Plato; Plato had a student named Aristotle; and Aristotle had a student named Alexander the Great. If you have the opportunity to ask any of our great leaders, I believe you will find that they are who they are because someone took the time to help them succeed.

Creating an Epiphanous Environment

Once again, epiphanies as I use them in this book are realizations that cause a person to change their behavior. So how do you create an environment that can foster epiphanies? The simple answer is one that causes someone to question their perception of reality, which is, I must say, much easier said than done.

To get someone to question and maybe change their perception of reality requires that you confront them with a situation that they have never faced before. This can be as simple as an idea or perspective that they have never considered or some life-changing event such as getting married, having a child, being promoted, etc. As leaders that are interested in developing other leaders, we can create situations, put forth ideas, and question a prospective leader's thoughts to get them to re-examine whether their perceptions are valid.

If we are their manager or mentor, we can place them into situations that they have never faced before and gauge their reactions. We can expose them to different perspectives around situations they may face. One way to do this is to ask them how they would handle a situation that *you* recently experienced. Another way is to provide an example of what other leaders have done in similar situations and ask their opinion. Find out what they would do in different situations by placing them into role-playing. Have them address conditions that they may have to face and then discuss what could have been done better. Guide them to leadership-based books, articles, research, and scholarly papers.

To create an epiphanous environment is to place the prospective leader into a learning mode. Make a place of learning for leadership; make time for reflection and thought. Give them homework that causes them to draw conclusions. Send them to see other leaders in action and report the results. Put them in a situation that requires they teach something they know little or nothing about so they have to master the subject enough to teach it.

Whenever a prospective leader fails at something, it creates a teachable moment. Take advantage of it. Glean what can be learned from the incident; develop an action plan and a way to prevent it from recurring again. Promulgate this gleaned information to the rest of the prospective leaders and mentors in the program. Share the learning.

> *"Leadership and learning are indispensable to each other."*
>
> *John F. Kennedy*

Into the Deep End of the Pool

Like most children, when I was learning to swim, I developed a fear of leaving the comfort and security of the edge or shore. But at some point we must all let go and swim in water that is over our heads if we are to truly learn to swim. It is the same with learning to lead. We need to be thrust into the deep end of the pool if we are to make progress.

Respect that learning leadership isn't necessarily a comfortable process. As we challenge prospective leaders to grasp and master the lessons of leadership, we must recognize that it is inappropriate to simply throw people into the deep end and hope they swim. Rather, we must provide some safeties in case of failure. I like to think of it as throwing someone in deep enough water that they have to swim yet providing a means to bounce off the bottom when necessary.

We create situations that provide opportunities for prospective leaders to stretch, move outside their comfort zones, and experience new and different situations. And it may be difficult to predict whether any of these situations will be pleasant learning experiences or difficult learning experiences. But regardless, prospective leaders need to learn the realities of leadership, from the great exuberances of success to the failures of management which result in laying people off or firing people. Learning leadership, after all, is about developing character.

When you do throw someone into the deep end of the pool, make sure they have a path for success. This path to success must be traveled by the prospective leader with as little help from others as possible. They have to find their own way for effective learning to occur and, as these things sometimes work out, both teacher and student may learn from the experience. The fact is that we only grow by reaching beyond our current abilities. But the lessons we learn by our own growth are the ones that we learn the best and retain the longest.

> *"Man cannot discover new oceans unless he has the courage to lose sight of the shore."*
>
> *Andre Gide*

Failure is a Part of Learning

We all experience failure in our lives. Whether learning to walk, learning to read, playing sports or reading music, we all failed, learned, and tried different things until we got it. I can't tell you all the times I failed to comprehend calculus; but when I finally looked at it from a different perspective, I began to understand it and did well in school.

Learning leadership is extremely complex. We are dealing with people, which are some of the most complex systems in the universe. No two people think alike, perceive the world in the same way, or process information in the same manner. I personally think it's a miracle that we can work together at all; but we do, and it is amazing sometimes what we can accomplish together.

The journey to leadership is fraught with failure. And it's only natural given that we frequently operate with imperfect situational awareness or must act on data and information that is incomplete or based on inaccurate assumptions. There is no such thing as perfect information when it comes to people and situations. In fact, even if we had perfect information about people and situations, we probably wouldn't have the capacity to evaluate it all. How could you evaluate the thoughts, perceptions, and desires of a hundred people, of thousands or more? Even limiting the topics to one or two, the task is unmanageable. But this is the reality we face as leaders.

We naturally categorize things as a way of dealing with our world. But this natural categorization also blinds us to things that could be important. With leaders, as with anyone else, there are things we pay attention to and things we don't. If necessary, we may compensate for the things we don't see by making assumptions. We extrapolate our perceptions into areas that we believe can still work. But as you might expect, a lot of times this doesn't work and we fail. There are a number of ways to fail; but the real opportunity is to explore this new unexamined area, learn from it, and, if necessary, change our perception of reality and our behavior. In short, we have an epiphany.

> *"Anyone who has never made a mistake has never tried anything new."*
>
> *Albert Einstein*

Dr. Phil McGraw from the television show *"Dr. Phil"* likes to ask the question, "How's that working for you?" I really like this question when working with prospective leaders – especially when you see that they are running into difficulties. It gets them to think about what they did, the results, and how they might do things differently in the future. It's important to build an environment where they can feel safe to try different things without the fear of reprisal. Prospective leaders need to be challenged and feel safe but yet know their limitations. They have to be able to jump into that deep end if they want to and still feel the support of their leaders and mentors.

Reinforcing Beneficial Behaviors

The teachers or mentors of prospective leaders need to reinforce beneficial behaviors when they see them just as you would with any student, with one notable exception – the reward is for beneficial behaviors exhibited by the prospective leader's organization or group as opposed to the behavior they personally exhibited. More simply, you look at the results of the prospective leader's behavior as to how it affected the group. Is the group inspired or de-motivated? Do they consistently innovate or are they reactionary? Is the group cohesive or fragmented? What behaviors by the leader led to these results? Was it what the leader expected or desired?

One of the issues prospective leaders need to recognize is that their behaviors may not elicit the same results each time. Nonetheless, they need to always bring out the best in their group. Is the prospective leader in touch with the group? Are they aware of the skills and resources they have available in the organization? Do they know when to ask for help? These are all good questions that can orient the prospective leader to refocus and experiment with how to lead.

Reinforcement need not take the form of actual rewards. Sincere appreciation is sometimes more helpful to motivate and reinforce desired behavior than receiving a reward. Make sure that your processes are vigilant enough to see the actions and the results near in time to when they take place. Nothing stings quite like extraordinary effort that goes unnoticed. Whatever the process, reinforcement of beneficial behavior needs to be immediate, appropriate, and specific.

Help Them Craft Their Vision

The most critical ability for a leader, even a prospective leader, is the ability to articulate a future state. As I mentioned in the traits that I look for in prospective leaders, this is not an optional skill. To effectively lead, a leader must be able to articulate and form specific images in the minds of people. The basic form is based in storytelling. Can the person use words to craft specific visions in the minds of the listener? We all can tell stories, but leaders must be very good at it.

Mentors and teachers can help prospective leaders develop this skill by asking them to describe some future in short stories. It doesn't matter whether it is about the lunch they are about to have or some global hope for world peace. The point is just to practice the telling. Ask questions: What does that look like and how do you envision it turning out? Make sure that they can describe your part in this future state, and make sure that their vision is believable and fully describes every aspect of the future state. Can they weave a story from others into their future vision? Practice weaving the story of Christopher Columbus and his arrival to the Americas as a stepping stone for the future vision they have. Just like any other skill, practice is needed to develop and excel.

To emphasize how important this skill is, I can only tell you that a prospective leader will not be successful without it. It is a skill that salespeople use to persuade others to buy their wares, politicians use to get votes, and great teachers use to inspire students. After all, great leaders are the purveyors of dreams and visions of the future.

Maintaining Contact

Many of the leadership training programs I have seen are one to two weeks long, and then you are on your own. If you learn nothing else from this book, I hope you understand that leadership is a lifelong journey. You cannot teach leadership in a few weeks or even in just a few years. I think of it as learning any other fine art – painting, music, dancing, or even writing. Learning leadership actually never stops. In this light, neither should the teaching of it. Leadership should be fostered and supported for as long as the person is in the organization – and even beyond that. Maintain contact.

Even if the person moves out of the organization, contact should still be maintained with their mentors and teachers. I know many who have left organizations only to return to them with much more experience and skill. People are not limited by organizational boundaries. People are loyal to people, especially to their teachers and mentors. Who knows? Your next CEO may come back to you after many years to lead the organization to new heights.

Demanding Standards

The leadership program needs to be demanding. Regardless of the level or experience, programs need to push a prospective leader's capabilities. It's how they grow. This attribute of the program mirrors the throwing-people-into-the-deep-end-of-the-pool philosophy previously discussed.

Admiral Rickover, the father of the U.S. Navy's nuclear power program, designed a training program that was very demanding regardless of the level or ability of the student. For the most part this was accomplished by tailoring the work and instruction to the student. Students with basic skills learned the fundamentals; students with advanced skills learned the fundamentals plus more complex concepts. If you were in Section 1, you were expected to be able to use the equations properly. If you were in Section 15, you were expected to derive them.

Every prospective leader is different, so your leadership program must be tailored to each individual. Each person learns at a different rate and has epiphanies at different rates. While each person has the ability to deal with change; depending on what is going on in their lives and what their needs are, the rate at which they accept and adapt to change may differ. Change is really what learning is about. The ability of a person to deal with change is directly proportional to their rate of learning. Push them. As leaders, they will experience the significant pressures of their position, and training methods need to help prepare them to cope with that.

Measure Progress

How do you measure the progress of a leader? The short answer is by measuring the change in behavior, just as we do with any other training. To do this, you specifically look for the behaviors that are associated with their leadership epiphanies. Each of these epiphanies actually causes some change in behavior which can be observed and measured. By observing either the prospective leader's behavior or the reflective behavior of their group or organization, you can understand which epiphany level they have reached.

In addition to the five main epiphanies, there are many other epiphanies leaders will experience. To understand the changes, the original behaviors need to be documented to develop a baseline. This can be done by simply asking questions and seeing what the person's thoughts are about situations that they may face and watching them in leadership situations. An organizational development specialist should be able to help develop the assessment tools.

Just like with other training, a task list of behaviors can be developed and a program can be implemented to teach the techniques and reinforce leadership philosophies. While learning techniques is a good thing, leaders must have a genuine understanding of human nature and the culture that they are working in. They can lead as the situation changes, as they face challenges that techniques haven't been developed for.

The old adage "What gets measured, gets done" is quite applicable to leadership training. When you measure the behavior changes, even by the act of paying attention to them, you affect the outcomes. Almost any person that is paid attention to will at some level be affected by the attention. In most cases, this will be positive; but it can turn negative if the attention turns to scrutiny and micro-management. So a balance between measuring progress and micro-monitoring must be struck. How do you know where to draw the line? Ask them. The simple act of asking the prospective leader how much feedback and observation they need will usually be the right amount.

What is acceptable progress? That is a good question, and I'm sorry that I don't have a definitive answer. This needs to be worked out between your prospective leader and the mentor or teachers. Remember that everyone has a certain level of change that they are willing to accept. Understand that I didn't say "feel comfortable with," but "willing to accept." We need to be demanding if real growth is to occur. Some people can progress through some epiphanies easily, while others may reach an epiphany and stop progressing altogether.

Widen the Circle

If people only learned from a single source, you would only have one perspective and our ability to envision different states would be stunted. This is one reason many universities have foreign campuses and promote exchange programs. It helps students understand about different cultures, values, and perspectives. Every leadership program needs to have this same capability.

Send prospective leaders to see firsthand how different successful leaders lead. Encourage them to watch what they do, understand why they do what they do, and learn how they inspire others. Sending prospective leaders to work with others within your company or organization is a start, but there are other ways to see very different leadership styles and activities. How about sending them to work with a political figure or the leader of one of your vendors or contracted firms? Exposure to leaders in public service – fire departments, police departments, or public works departments – can have a lasting impact on a prospective leader. Every leader must answer to someone. Learning this by observing who others answer to and how they succeed in their environments can be enlightening and very educational. It could even cause epiphanies to occur. After all, isn't that what we are trying to accomplish?

> *"Management is about arranging and telling.*
> *Leadership is about nurturing and enhancing."*
>
> *Tom Peters*

Perpes

For those who don't know what "perpes" is, it is the Latin word for "never-ending." The quest to find and develop leaders is never-ending. Leaders develop the power to shape perceptions, create inspiring visions, and provide the example of what we should be. Notice that I didn't say they knew the path to achieving that vision. In many cases they don't, but they inspire people to find those paths.

The path of the leader is one of continuous learning. People, after all, are the subject of study and they are about as close to an infinite subject as I know. We will never know everything about people or even a single individual, let alone ourselves. Because leadership is about people, it too is a never-ending subject of study.

A final thought…

You teach by actions. Teaching by actions is the most effective way to shape perceptions. Like a picture says more than a thousand words, actions speak volumes. If nothing else, prospective leaders must learn that their actions are what counts in the end. When we look back at great leaders, we hear their words – but only because their deeds warranted our attention first.

Selection and Care of Prospective Leaders

"In reading the lives of great men, I found that the first victory they won was over themselves ... self-discipline with all of them came first."

Harry S. Truman

Chapter 9

Recognizing the Journey

Setting out on the path to become a leader is a conscious decision that every leader has made for themselves. While some say that leaders are chosen, the fact is that leaders usually make the decision to lead. Sometimes we make that decision without a full understanding of the situation, but we make it nonetheless. We are not all successful. In fact, none of us are successful all the time. Every leader has faced failure. What made them successful is how they overcame failure and continued on.

A Journey of Persistence

You can look at the people that we consider great leaders and see that they all overcame adversity. Some may have been born into a leadership position while others had their own demons, distractions, and a host of other issues to conquer to become the leaders we admire and read about. If you think about it, leaders face challenges every day. From picking their successor to dealing with moral issues, deciding to lay off people to deciding whom to promote, there are a myriad of issues and decisions that leaders encounter daily. Each is an opportunity to be the example of what the leader values and to move their organizations closer to the vision.

"The problem is not that there are problems. The problem is expecting otherwise and thinking that having problems is a problem."

Theodore Rubin

Leadership requires strength – strength in your convictions, your values, and your beliefs for the future. As the leader, you must carry on many times in the face of opposition. You may present a logical argument but be faced with opposition that is based on someone else's beliefs. These are actually the hardest objections to overcome, if they can be overcome at all.

At times in your career, you may find that you have more information or a better understanding of a subject than someone with the power to make the decision. And despite that you have kept people properly informed and educated, you may need to summon the strength to make a decision and later ask for forgiveness rather than to wait and ask for permission.

There is no telling what circumstance you will encounter, but all leaders face opposition. You must draw strength from your own convictions and remain firm in your beliefs and vision at these times.

"Courage isn't having the strength to go on – it is going on when you don't have strength."

Napoleon Bonaparte

A Journey of Trust

"Trust is the essence of leadership."

Colin Powell

Three types of trust help us lead – the trust our people have in our ability to lead, the trust we have in our people, and the trust we have in ourselves. A leader must have all three to be successful.

To gain the trust of our people, we need to show that we will do what we say we are going to do. When our actions reflect what we say, we gain the reputation of being dependable. It's really not a hard concept to grasp, but the implementation can sometimes tell the true character of a person.

Take the situation where a New York City detective told a waitress that her tip was half of his winnings of a lotto ticket. While the actual circumstances were much different than the movie *"It Could Happen To You"* portrays, the officer and the waitress actually did split the $6 million winning ticket. Robert Cunningham didn't have to tell her that he held the winning ticket. The ticket is, after all, a bearing instrument and whoever holds it is the legal owner. He could have simply said that it was not the winning ticket or that it won just a couple of dollars. Instead, he did what he said he would do and split the prize. Imagine the level of trust this action fostered in the detective by his keeping his word.

Leaders must also trust their people. As leaders, we trust them with our reputations, our careers, and sometimes with our very lives. I spent several years on submarines, and each of us had to trust that the other members of the crew would perform their jobs carefully and admirably every day. Any mistake could spell disaster for the entire crew at any time. Whereas this level of trust may not reflect your everyday existence, it is a rather impressive example considering that the average age of the crew is in the low 20s.

US Navy Official Photo

Lastly, a leader must trust themselves. They must trust in their personal values, vision, and direction. They must trust that they are doing the right things and they must trust in their ability to turn the vision into a reality. Without this trust in self, there can be no real leadership.

On the journey to becoming a great leader, we must foster trust in our people, learn how to give trust, and learn to trust ourselves – and we must learn that trust for the most part is not given, it is earned.

"Trust men and they will be true to you: treat them greatly and they will show themselves great."

Ralph Waldo Emerson

A Journey of Patience

Becoming a leader is a lot like climbing Mount Everest. It's a challenging endeavor, to say the least. But climbing Mount Everest is accomplished in the same way by all who attempt it – one step at a time. We have our first epiphanies and it changes our behavior; this causes us to see things with new perspective, which in turn prepares us to experience the next epiphany. True, we may understand the epiphanies and what they mean – we may even be able to mimic the actions – but unless we have had a true epiphany that changes the way we think, which in turn reflects a change in our values, we will be nothing more than great actors. Great leaders, on the other hand, are authentic and that comes from developing values and a vision for the future that permeates every part of their lives.

"Good ideas are not adopted automatically. They must be driven into practice with courageous patience."

Hyman Rickover

It takes time to learn leadership. Even if you are thrown into a position of leadership, you will still need time to learn how to lead. Trust is earned, and earning that trust takes time as well. You must learn to be patient with yourself as you learn, observe, and practice the actions of a leader. You will need time to craft and to articulate a great vision that others can envision and buy into with heart and mind. You will need time to understand people and how they work within social settings. We also hope that we have chosen and been chosen by mentors that will be patient with us as we become great leaders in our own right.

Patience is a quality we need as we lead too. We must have patience with our people because they need time to experience their own epiphanies about the vision and future that you have presented. We need to be patient as they change and learn, and this patience should be proportional to the amount and rate of change that we ask of them.

"Patience is necessary, and one cannot reap immediately where one has sown."

Soren Kierkegaard

A Journey of Relationships

"The most important single ingredient in the formula of success is knowing how to get along with people."

Theodore Roosevelt

I know of no leader of people that did not build relationships with people first. If you think about it, leadership is a very special kind of relationship. It is about the give and take with a group of people that can create something very special.

On our journey to becoming leaders, we have many relationships. Some of them have helped us understand our visions and helped us define what we are about. Some relationships have taught us the capacity for nobility and treachery within the human condition. We learn that some relationships are conditional and some are altruistic. We learn to value some relationships for a lifetime, regardless of how long they actually lasted.

284

None of us become leaders without great relationships that guided us, comforted us, and mentored us. These relationships are to be valued, appreciated, and cherished. We owe a debt of gratitude for these relationships that we know we will never be able to repay. I know that I could never repay my father for the lessons he taught me.

We discover that every relationship can teach us something, and we need to appreciate that it is the relationships we have that cause us to have epiphanies in the first place. In fact, I have observed that the closer the relationship, the more likely that relationship will cause an epiphany in our lives. But even relationships that are one-sided can cause us to have epiphanies. While I never met Stephen Covey, Tom Peters, or Harry Truman, their thoughts and philosophies certainly changed my perspective and caused me to experience epiphanies. The way they documented their relational experiences rings of truth and enlightenment to me, and I can relate to their situations.

Leaders give hope. Leaders give a vision of what the future could be. Leaders take the organization's energy and focus it on a goal. Leaders take the group's enthusiasm and output and reflect it out to the world to attract resources. It is a dynamic relationship, marked by a constant give and take between the leader and the group.

> *"We make a living by what we get; we make a life by what we give."*
>
> *Winston Churchill*

A Journey with a Destination

The journey of becoming a leader does have a destination; but like the summit of Mount Everest, the destination is not the end of our journey, but a milestone of becoming who we are to become. Most great leaders don't become leaders for the sake of being a leader, but to achieve some greater purpose. President Reagan didn't grow up thinking or desiring to become president, but became one as a means of implementing his vision for the people of the United States. He saw a need and used the presidency as a means to fulfill that need.

When Steve Jobs was growing up, he didn't think, "I want to be the leader of one of the most innovative, game-changing companies in the world." He loved tinkering with things. He admired the elegance of form and how technology could intersect with that. Becoming a leader was a means to an end. I'm assuming that Herb Kelleher was not thinking that he would change the aviation industry when he started law school; but when he became a leader, he did exactly that. If you think about the great leaders in our history, most of them never had the intention to become a great leader for the sake of being a leader, but rather to do something great; leadership was a means to an end.

So if you are thinking that leadership is the destination, you are mistaken. You must have a great goal or vision. That is the true destination.

> *"All you need is the plan, the road map, and the courage to press on to your destination."*
>
> *Earl Nightingale*

A Journey of Triumphs and Failures

The journey to becoming a leader is a personal one. We have company that can help us and provide us with examples, but we must make the trek ourselves. We must make the mistakes and learn from them ourselves. We may take a moment to look back and see our progress; but in the end, we know the triumphs and failures of the journey more intensely than anyone else because they are personal to us.

"Not in the shouts and plaudits of the throng, but in ourselves, are triumph and defeat."

Henry Wadsworth Longfellow

It's interesting that what we read about in the news are the great triumphs and failures of our leaders. We rarely see what it has actually taken to get to that point. Leaders don't wake up one day and decide to have a triumphant moment or dismal failure; they journey to those moments just like the rest of us. We walk a path that we see as one that will get us to our vision; we take it one step at a time hoping that it gets us to where we want to be. There is always the element of uncertainty in what we do as leaders. We actually never know with certainty what will transpire or how things will turn out. This uncertainty is what makes leadership exciting to some and brings consternation to others. But if you think about it, if everything were a certainty, would it be worth pursuing?

"Without the element of uncertainty, the bringing off of even the greatest business triumph would be dull, routine, and eminently unsatisfying."

J. Paul Getty

One thing that we can all be sure about as leaders is that there will be failure. We have witnessed it, experienced it, caused it, and benefited by it. Failure is a defining human characteristic. As leaders, we learn from failure; but even more so, we overcome failure to develop success. We understand that failures are opportunities to refine our processes and tactics. Consider how universal the concept of failure is in human understanding. Failure is one of the truths in humanity.

"Develop success from failures. Discouragement and failure are two of the surest stepping stones to success."

Dale Carnegie

"Failure is the key to success; each mistake teaches us something."

Morihei Ueshiba

When you think about it, reveling in the triumphs of the organization must be a celebration of what *they* did. After all, the leader's real job was to provide the vision. Our triumph can only be that we were successful in inspiring the right people at the right moment in time. My advice to leaders is never to think that what has been done was done by you but, rather, to remember that it has been done by your people.

"No man will make a great leader who wants to do it all himself or get all the credit for doing it."

Andrew Carnegie

A Journey of Epiphanies...

Some say that leaders are born; others say leaders learn their craft. I believe that leaders are made – some by their situations, some by other leaders, and some by desire. All leaders have epiphanies on their journey to becoming great leaders. I don't think people are born with all the knowledge or skill to be leaders; they must experience the human condition to know whom it is they lead. But as the proverbial saying goes, you can lead a horse to water, but you can't make it drink. And so it is with epiphanies. You can bring a person to the brink of an epiphany, but they may not yet be ready to accept the different perception of reality.

All leaders must have these epiphanies. Some come to them naturally or, rather, their life situations make it possible for them to have them at an early age and to absorb their meaning and adjust their thinking and life.

You cannot do everything yourself; you must let others help you – the first epiphany any leader experiences. This is actually the first step to becoming a leader. This one realization sets you on the journey, so long as you are ready to go there.

At some point you realize that it doesn't have to be done your way; it can be done *their* way and still meet the expectations – the second epiphany. This is your first inclination that people are a great asset and have value.

With the third epiphany, you realize that everyone is smarter than you on some level. What a great discovery. Everyone can contribute something!

With the fourth epiphany, you come to realize that your job is actually to help people become successful. How you do that depends on the situation.

The fifth epiphany that can be learned at any time is that all you really have is influence. So you discover ways to influence and inspire.

The road to leadership is not what we aspire to normally. It is, rather, a combination of situations that directs us to it. We develop great passions and, with that, we create great visions that inspire others. We are compelled to learn about people and how best to help others participate to reach our vision. And along this journey are great discoveries and insights which must be passed on to others so that the cycle of human advancement can continue. The epiphanies are but the unspoken transformations that occur in our hearts and minds as we journey. And as we journey, we learn, we teach, and rejoice in the meaning of our realized visions.

> *"Some of us have great runways already built for us. If you have one, take off. But if you don't have one, realize it is your responsibility to grab a shovel and build one for yourself and for those who will follow after you."*

> *Amelia Earhart*

Bibliography

(n.d.). Retrieved June 7, 2012, from www.onlinecollege.com: http://www.onlinecollege.org/2010/02/16/50-famously-successful-people-who-failed-at-first/

(n.d.). Retrieved September 4, 2012, from www.dictionary.com: http://dictionary.reference.com

(n.d.). Retrieved 10 30, 2012, from Merriam-Webster.com: http://www.merriam-webster.com/dictionary/leadership

(2012, June 17). Retrieved July 1, 2012, from Wikipedia.org: http://en.wikipedia.org/wiki/Synergy

Covey, S. R. (1989). *Seven Habits of Highly Effective People.* New York: Free Press.

Harvey, J. B. (1974, summer). The Abilene paradox: the management of agreement. *Organizational Dynamics 3*, 63-80.

Report: Japan, utility at fault for response to nuclear disaster. (2011, December 26). *LA Times* .

Rogers, D. (2005, November 13). *Answers to Big Three's "Black October" Are People, Says Pat Carrigan.* Retrieved May 11, 2013, from mybaycity.com: http://mybaycity.mmcctech.net/scripts/p3_v2/P3V3-0200.cfm?P3_newspaperID=NewspaperID&P3_ArticleID=934

Schneider, D. &. (1998). Be a model leader of change. *Management Review, Vol. 87, Issue 3*, 41-46.

Bibliography

Sports Reference LLC. (n.d.). *Teams*. Retrieved July 15, 2011, from www.baseball-reference.com: http://www.baseball-reference.com/teams/

Stuart, R. (1995). The outcomes and influencing factors of change. *Personnel Review Vol. 24, Issue 2*, 53-85.

Sweeney, D. (2000). The Challenge of Perpetual Change. *Management Review Vol. 89, Issue 2*, 46.

The American Heritage Dictionary of the English Language, Fourth Edition. (2009). New York: Houghton Mifflin Company.

Zimmerman, J. (1995). The principles of managing change. *HR Focus Vol. 72, Issue 2*, 15-17.

www.ingramcontent.com/pod-product-compliance
Lightning Source LLC
Chambersburg PA
CBHW020605270326
41927CB00005B/183